Instructive Chess Miniatures

Alper Efe Ataman

T0266169

ISBN-13: 978-1-910093-88-7
ISBN-10: 1-910093-88-2

DISTRIBUTION:
Worldwide (except USA): Central Books Ltd, 99 Wallis Rd, London E9 5LN, England.
Tel +44 (0)20 8986 4854 Fax +44 (0)20 8533 5821. E-mail: orders@Centralbooks.com

Gambit Publications Ltd, 99 Wallis Rd, London E9 5LN, England.
E-mail: info@gambitbooks.com
Website (regularly updated): www.gambitbooks.com

Edited by Graham Burgess
Typeset by Petra Nunn
Cover image by Andrés Guadalupe Martín
Printed in the USA by Bang Printing, Brainerd, Minnesota

10 9 8 7 6 5 4 3 2 1

Gambit Publications Ltd
Directors: Dr John Nunn GM, Murray Chandler GM, and Graham Burgess FM
German Editor: Petra Nunn WFM

Contents

Symbols

+	check	??	blunder
++	double check	0-0	castles kingside
x	captures	0-0-0	castles queenside
#	checkmate	1-0	The game ends in a win for White
!!	brilliant move	½-½	The game ends in a draw
!	good move	0-1	The game ends in a win for Black
!?	interesting move	Ch	Championship
?!	dubious move	(*n*)	*n*th match game
?	bad move	(*D*)	see next diagram

Bibliography

Books

Attack and Defence, Mark Dvoretsky and Artur Yusupov, Batsford 1998
Beating 1 e4 e5 – A Repertoire for White in the Open Games, John Emms, Everyman 2010
Build Up Your Chess 2, Artur Yusupov, Quality Chess 2008
Chess Brilliancy, Yakov Damsky, Everyman 2002
Chess Training for Post-Beginners, Yaroslav Srokovski, New in Chess 2014
Chinese School of Chess, Liu Wenzhe, Batsford 2002
Garry Kasparov's Greatest Chess Games Volume 1, Igor Stohl, Gambit Publications 2005
Judit Polgar Teaches Chess 1: How I Beat Fischer's Record, Judit Polgar, Quality Chess 2012
The Mammoth Book of the World's Greatest Chess Games (3rd edition), Graham Burgess,
    John Nunn and John Emms, Constable and Robinson 2010
Mastering Opening Strategy, Johan Hellsten, Everyman 2012
Satrançta Sistematik Antrenman (*Das Systematische Schachtraining* – Edition Olms),
    Sergiu Samarian, İnkilap Kitabevi 1991
Starting Out: King's Indian Attack, John Emms, Everyman 2005

Periodicals

Inside Chess (various issues)
New in Chess (various issues)

Digital Sources

Mega Database 2014, ChessBase GmbH
www.chessgames.com
Ustalar Nasıl Kazanıyor 1-5 (How Masters Win 1-5), Selim Gürcan, www.satrancokulu.com
Wikipedia, The Free Encyclopedia

Foreword

As a chess enthusiast, I have always admired chess masters and authors for their efforts. Although their guiding works are only small reflections of their collected experience over the years, the dedication and endeavour are priceless.

In my home country of Turkey, I have published and presented many chess books for chess lovers of all levels. I am not sure whether this is a success story, but for me, the excitement has always been my main source of motivation. In order to be truly successful, one should continuously challenge oneself by setting new goals. This approach is the only way to keep our enthusiasm alive. After spending substantial amounts of time with up-and-coming chess-players, and also examining many types of chess books, I really wanted to write a good chess book myself. That's how the idea for *Instructive Chess Miniatures* was born.

But why miniatures? It's a known fact that instructive games are basic resources for improving young chess-players, or in other words *masters of the future*. Battles between two equally-strong players are often quite long with many subtle points and a variety of themes. This makes them harder work to study, especially for younger players who may lose their focus on the main theme. Miniatures, however, last at most for 25 moves. These short games usually come to an end with a spectacular combination, or an admirable deep idea. This makes miniatures really amazing and memorable!

I am sure that you are quite familiar with some of the examples presented in the book. I have included some of the great classics, as, in my humble opinion, every chess enthusiast should know them by heart. Still, I believe that you will also find some unknown games, which, I hope, will make you as thrilled as I was after analysing them.

Besides miniatures, I have tried to emphasize the key points by presenting some similar cases from the past and the future. This way, I have aimed to show how chess miniatures can be inspiring for the next generations.

I hope that all readers will enjoy *Instructive Chess Miniatures*, and I will be particularly happy if this book manages to attract youngsters to the fascinating world of chess.

The Evergreen Game

Game 1

Anderssen – Dufresne

Berlin 1852

Evans Gambit

1 e4 e5 2 ♘f3 ♘c6 3 ♗c4 ♗c5 4 b4 *(D)*

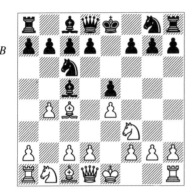

This is the *Evans Gambit*. In this opening system, White sacrifices a pawn (or two) in order to attain a lead in development and seize the initiative. If Black replies carelessly, these factors can quickly become overwhelming in the initial stage of the game. If Black accepts the pawn, White will gain time to set up a pawn-centre with c3 and d4, and this is the main strategic idea behind White's gambit. Still, just like many other gambits, it should be mentioned that the gambiteer takes on significant risks by accepting a material deficit.

4...♗xb4

When facing a gambit, the most natural reaction is to accept the sacrificed material. Then at least you will have a material advantage to compensate for the opponent's upcoming pressure, and may be able to return the material to defuse it at a later point. Still, the more solid 4...♗b6 is a viable alternative.

5 c3 ♗a5 6 d4

Black chose 5...♗a5 in order to pin the c3-pawn after a possible d4 push. Alas, Anderssen continues to advance his pawns without any hesitation. An initiative (by which we mean 'the ability to create threats') is a temporary

advantage for its possessor. In order not to lose this important element, it is more or less an obligation to continue with moves that leave the opponent only with forced replies.

6...exd4 7 0-0 *(D)*

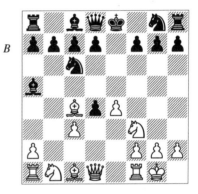

7...d3

Black aims to deny White's queenside pieces a quick route into battle. Thus he is willing to return a pawn, in order to keep some lines closed for the time being. This type of approach is typical: sometimes in order to neutralize the opponent's onslaught, part of the material advantage can be given back. On the other hand, the way Black has chosen to do so here costs time in itself, and White is by no means obliged to spend a move capturing the pawn on d3.

Indeed, Anderssen is not interested in winning a pawn back. Over the next few moves, he brings some 'heavy artillery' into his attack.

8 ♕b3 ♕f6 9 e5 ♕g6 10 ♖e1 ♘ge7 11 ♗a3

White has brought his pieces quickly into battle, putting pressure on Black's king, which is still in the centre. So far, the game has been developing quite normally, as Black, in his turn, develops his knight right after solidifying the f7-pawn with his queen.

But right at this moment, Dufresne makes an interesting decision, with the aim of bringing his undeveloped rook and bishop into the game. I'm quite sure that modern players of our era would consider this enterprising attempt rather inappropriate.

11...b5?!

This kind of a sacrifice against an almost-developed army is certainly risky. True, White is forced to accept this sacrifice, and this brings White's initiative to a temporary halt. However, it seems highly improbable that the time Black gains is sufficient to justify the loss of a pawn and the damage to his queenside structure. 11...d5 is a better move, for instance.

12 ♕xb5 ♖b8 13 ♕a4 ♗b6 14 ♘bd2 ♗b7 *(D)*

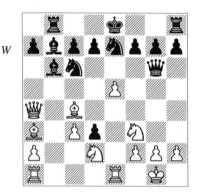

Black may have been seeking to reach this position with his risky pawn sacrifice. His queen exerts some pressure along the g-file and his bishops are also targeting White's kingside. However, one crucial element is missing in Black's counterplay: the *initiative*. At the moment Anderssen is aware that his opponent does not yet possess any concrete threats. Consequently, White is first to launch his attack:

15 ♘e4!

Compared to other pieces, knights are rather short-range forces; they are most effective when they are close to the enemy camp. After 15 ♘e4, the defence of the d3-pawn has been cut off, and more importantly, ♘d6+ and ♘f6+ suddenly appear as dangerous ideas.

15...♕f5?! *(D)*

A sign of bad planning by Black. A more resilient defence is 15...d2, seeking to defuse

White's initiative by making him retreat his centralized knight. However, while this increases Black's chances of surviving the next few moves, White would still have a significant advantage.

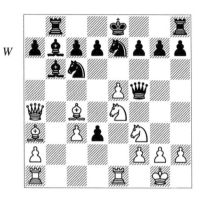

16 ♗xd3 ♕h5

The aforementioned ♘d6+/♘f6+ threats have forced Black to make another move with his queen.

White now has a number of promising options, of which Anderssen chooses the most spectacular, even if it is not the most convincing.

17 ♘f6+?! *(D)*

Of course, opening lines against an uncastled king is in general a very natural and effective approach. But in such an advantageous position, taking unnecessary risks may not be the most logical decision. *Simple chess* with, for instance, 17 ♘g3! ♕h6 18 ♗c1 ♕e6 19 ♗c4 is a way for White to make decisive material gains.

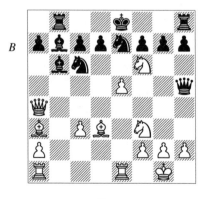

17...gxf6 18 exf6 ♖g8

Now the drawback of 17 ♘f6+?! can be seen clearly: Black suddenly has real counterplay along the g-file. In his turn, White needs to find a resourceful counter to his opponent's obvious idea – ...♕xf3.

19 ♖ad1!

When facing the opponent's threat, it is actually a fundamental mistake to look only for a way to fend it off. The ideal response is to find a way in which we can ignore the threat and instead implement our own ideas. In our case, Anderssen does not limit himself to the duty of defending the f3-knight. The German master instead prepares a much more effective threat of his own.

19...♕xf3? *(D)*

Failing to see White's deeply concealed idea, Black allows a mating combination. Several other moves have been analysed extensively here, with 19...♗d4! and 19...♕h3! both established as leading to a draw with correct play.

20 ♖xe7+!

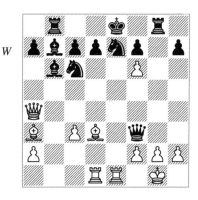

After centralizing both rooks, the lines to the black king must be cleared!

20...♘xe7 21 ♕xd7+!!

Now is the time to open the diagonals and implement some 'double check' ideas.

21...♔xd7 22 ♗f5++ ♔e8

22...♔c6 23 ♗d7#.

23 ♗d7+ ♔f8 24 ♗xe7# (1-0)

Inescapable Pins

Game 2
Schulten – Morphy
New York 1857
King's Gambit

1 e4 e5 2 f4 *(D)*

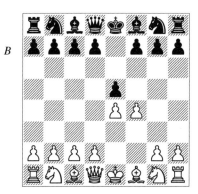

With the *King's Gambit*, White seeks to open the f-file and divert the black pawn from the centre. If Black fails to react to his opponent's 'offer' reasonably, White will acquire a strong pawn-centre, in addition to attacking

chances along the half-open f-file. Just like many other gambit systems, the main options for Black are either accepting or rejecting the sacrifice. But in this case, Morphy comes up with a distinctive alternative: offering a pawn sacrifice of his own!

2...d5!?

Black replies with the *Falkbeer Counter-Gambit*. The tension between the central pawns is increased, and this immediately sharpens the character of the game. Morphy chooses an option which offers him active piece-play, rather than 2...exf4, which gives him a pawn advantage. In the latter case, Black might face some unpleasant pressure from his opponent.

3 exd5 e4

Black's core concept: there are no obstacles for Black's active piece-play, while the pawn's presence on e4 controls f3 and limits White's active possibilities, as does White's own pawn on f4.

4 ♘c3?!

Sometimes in order to understand the drawbacks of seemingly natural moves, we need the help of classical games such as this one. Modern opening theory recommends immediately challenging the e4-pawn with 4 d3!. We shall see that attacking the pawn with 4 ♘c3 allows Black more serious counterplay, thanks to the possibility of pinning this knight with ...♗b4.

4...♘f6 5 d3 ♗b4 *(D)*

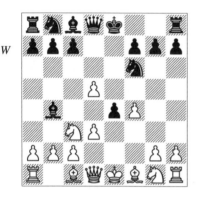

Black develops his bishop and keeps control of the e4-square with the help of the pin. In his turn, Schulten decides that the e4-pawn is the main inconvenience in his position, and in order to eliminate the pawn, unpins the knight with his bishop.

6 ♗d2 e3! *(D)*

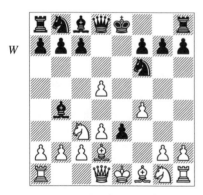

Breaking this pin is not that easy! Sometimes in the opening phase, the gambiteer faces a critical moment: in order to retain his initiative, it might be necessary to make additional

sacrifices. As the degree of risk increases with each new 'investment', it can prove quite hard for the gambiteer to decide on the right direction.

In our case, Morphy realizes the importance of maintaining the pin and he does not hesitate to sacrifice another pawn to reach his goal.

7 ♗xe3 0-0 *(D)*

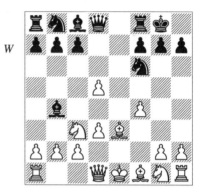

Now is a good moment to evaluate the position. Facing his opponent's sacrifices, White has had little choice but to spend time eliminating these pawns. As a result, his kingside is undeveloped and his king is stuck in the centre. Considering the pressure along the e-file, in addition to the pin on c3 and the black pieces' easy development, we can state that Black has acquired significant advantages in return for his sacrificed material.

8 ♗d2

Schulten decides to spend more time retreating his bishop. While White would prefer to develop, the natural 8 ♘f3? allows Black to increase his advantage substantially: 8...♖e8 9 ♕d2 ♗xc3! 10 bxc3 ♘xd5 and material losses cannot be avoided.

8...♗xc3

This exchange is consistent with Black's aims: by leaving the opponent only with forced replies, he retains the initiative.

9 bxc3 ♖e8+ 10 ♗e2 ♗g4

At this moment, most of us would expect the game to continue with 10...♘xd5. However, White's kingside is still undeveloped, and Morphy tries to benefit from this temporary fact by creating another pin along the d1-h5 diagonal, while at the same time preventing ♘f3.

11 c4 *(D)*

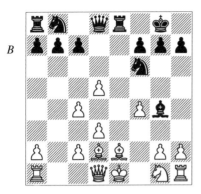

White's sole trump in the position is his material advantage. Therefore, he wants to protect his d5-pawn.

11...c6!

An outstanding move. The b8-knight is the only piece that has not been working in Black's team. Instead of simple development with ...♘bd7, Morphy seeks to bring this piece to its ideal position, namely the d4-square.

12 dxc6?

A chess miniature can only emerge with the 'cooperation' of both sides. A couple of moves ago, Schulten was willing to give back his d5-pawn in order to avoid greater problems. Now, given a chance, he exchanges this pawn, instead of losing it. However, this materialistic approach helps Black's knight join the battle effectively. 12 h3 is far more resilient.

12...♘xc6 13 ♔f1 *(D)*

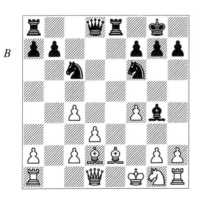

Another attempt to escape from a pin.

13...♖xe2!

No escape whatsoever! Whenever White has tried to break a pin, he has faced a sacrifice from his opponent. The c6-knight already has its eyes set on d4, and after this exchange sacrifice, the pin along the d1-h5 diagonal can rightly be called decisive.

14 ♘xe2 ♘d4

It is now impossible to endure the pressure on e2.

15 ♕b1 ♗xe2+ 16 ♔f2 ♘g4+ 17 ♔g1 *(D)*

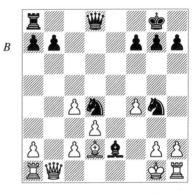

After a series of forced moves, Black just needs to find one more sacrifice to bring down his opponent's defence. We are past the point of positional evaluation; it is now time to calculate some specific tactics.

17...♘f3+!

This effective check both clears the d4-square for the queen and exposes White's king.

18 gxf3 ♕d4+ *(D)*

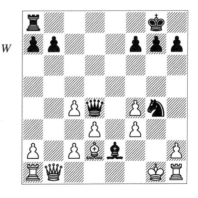

19 ♔g2 ♕f2+ 20 ♔h3 ♕xf3+ 21 ♔h4 ♘h6

Creating the threat of immediate mate by 22...♕g4#.

22 ♕g1 ♘f5+ 23 ♔g5 ♕h5# (0-1)

The Opera Game

Game 3
Morphy – Duke of Brunswick and Count Isouard
Paris 1858
Philidor Defence

1 e4 e5 2 ♘f3 d6 3 d4 ♗g4?!

As a general opening principle, one should give priority to developing pieces whose ideal squares have already been clarified. This way, we can avoid revealing our own plans at an early stage, and can develop the remaining pieces to squares where they best counter the opponent's set-up. Maybe former World Champion Lasker made his famous statement "get the knights into action, before both bishops are developed" in the light of classical games such as this one. In general, knights have fewer squares to choose from than bishops in the opening, so it is generally easier to identify their 'ideal squares'.

Returning to the game, we now see Black trying to protect his e5-pawn indirectly, by pinning the knight. But this effort is certainly unsuccessful, since White immediately seizes the initiative. Morphy does not want to give his opponents a wide range of options. Thus, he initiates a series of forced moves.

4 dxe5 ♗xf3

This exchange is forced; otherwise Black would lose a pawn without getting any compensation: 4...dxe5? 5 ♕xd8+ (unpinning the knight) 5...♔xd8 6 ♘xe5, with a decisive advantage to White.

5 ♕xf3 dxe5 *(D)*

It is true that Black has managed to avoid the loss of the pawn. But now the white pieces will simply join the game with tempo, and Morphy will attain a substantial lead in development.

6 ♗c4 ♘f6 7 ♕b3

Of course, it is contrary to opening principles to move the queen twice when there are still some undeveloped pieces. But sometimes in chess, concrete goals in the struggle take priority ahead of every other consideration. Here, White attacks the b7- and f7-pawns at the same time, and this disrupts his opponents' development.

7...♕e7 8 ♘c3!?

An exchange of queens would severely reduce the chances of White launching a successful mating attack, so Morphy avoids grabbing the pawn with 8 ♕xb7, which could be met by 8...♕b4+. That said, this leaves White a solid pawn ahead with an undoubtedly winning endgame. Instead, he wants to overwhelm Black (who suffers severely from a lack of development) by throwing more force into the battle.

8...c6

The right way to defend the pawn: at the same time, Black deprives the white knight of its desired ♘d5 ideas.

9 ♗g5 b5? *(D)*

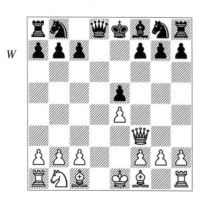
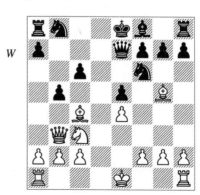

Such careless play definitely deserves punishment. According to Steinitz's principles "in chess only the attacker wins; but the right to attack is enjoyed **only** by the player who has the better position". Groundless assaults in inferior positions can only worsen the situation.

Black is without his light-squared bishop, following his 4th move, ...♗xf3. Given that he is already vulnerable on the light squares, this aggressive pawn-push, which weakens the light squares further without even trying to catch up with his development, invites a violent response.

10 ♘xb5!

Now it is time to rise up to the challenge. This knight sacrifice creates trouble for Black's uncastled king along the a4-e8 diagonal.

10...cxb5 11 ♗xb5+ ♘bd7 12 0-0-0

Now we see the core idea behind Morphy's decision to delay castling. The pressure against the pinned d7-knight is felt more and more strongly.

12...♖d8 *(D)*

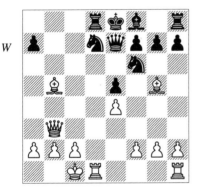

At some point in the battle, it is necessary to use tactical means to transform the strategic advantages that have been gained by locating pieces on their ideal positions. Here Morphy realizes that the rook on h1 is his only piece that is not contributing to his assault. And he cleverly finds a swift way to use this piece in his attack.

13 ♖xd7! ♖xd7 14 ♖d1

Thus White's undeveloped h1-rook has been 'exchanged' for a key defender: Black's d7-knight. Bound hand and foot, Black seeks to castle as quickly as possible. But this is a futile effort.

14...♛e6

Finally clearing the bishop's diagonal.

15 ♗xd7+ ♘xd7 *(D)*

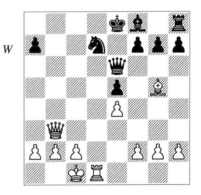

Morphy now finds an elegant way to clear the d-file. And the final blow belongs to... the formerly ineffective h1-rook!

16 ♛b8+! ♘xb8 17 ♖d8# (1-0)

Fury of the Hanging Queen

Game 4

Reiner – Steinitz

Vienna 1860

Scotch Gambit

1 e4 e5 2 ♘f3 ♘c6 3 d4 exd4 4 ♗c4

The *Scotch Gambit*. In this variation, White doesn't seek an opening advantage by building a pawn-centre with c3 and d4. Instead, he grounds his ambitions on rapid development and active piece-play. The course of the game will be more or less determined by Black's reaction.

4...♗c5 *(D)*

Attacking the remaining pawn in the centre with 4...♘f6 is the main alternative.

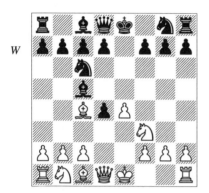

5 0-0

When we decide upon our opening set-ups, the general advice is to give priority to natural development. But in some opening lines a different philosophy is more appropriate, and we should seek to exploit specific or fleeting nuances. Here the c5-bishop is loose, and 5 c3 is an option that White might consider. For instance, 5...dxc3 6 ♗xf7+! ♔xf7 7 ♕d5+ gives White the upper hand as the black king is exposed and has lost its castling rights. Still, Black is not obliged to accept the pawn, and may instead transpose to Giuoco Piano waters with 5...♘f6.

5...d6

A risky but ambitious decision from the very first World Champion: instead of seeking safety on the kingside with ...♘f6 followed by ...0-0, Black aims to pin the f3-knight by ...♗g4. The well-analysed line 5...♘f6 6 e5 d5 7 exf6 dxc4 is called the *Max Lange Attack*, with 8 ♖e1+ ♗e6 9 ♘g5 ♕d5 10 ♘c3 ♕f5 11 ♘ce4 0-0-0 a possible continuation.

6 c3 ♗g4 7 ♕b3

Noticing that he can create a double attack on b7 and f7, Reiner escapes the pin immediately.

7...♗xf3

Challenging White's idea: instead of solidifying f7 with 7...♕d7, Steinitz proceeds with his own plan of breaking up his opponent's kingside structure.

8 ♗xf7+ ♔f8 9 ♗xg8?! *(D)*

The immediate 9 gxf3 is preferable.

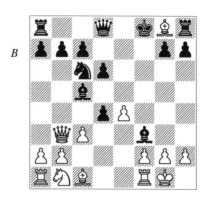

9...♖xg8 10 gxf3

After a series of more or less forced moves, the critical position has been reached. In the process, both kings' positions have been weakened. Trying to benefit from his opponent's disharmonious position, Black finds an extraordinary way to attack. The main motivation for his aggression is the lack of defenders on White's kingside, which is due to his undeveloped queenside and the queen's foray to b3.

10...g5! *(D)*

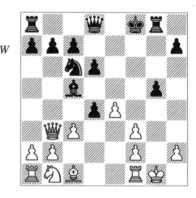

The factors supporting this apparently awkward move are the black rook being on g8 and the exposure of White's king along the g-file after 10 gxf3. Steinitz's idea is to clear the g-file for his rook with a timely ...g4 push.

11 ♕e6 ♘e5!

It is highly improbable that the white queen's penetration into Black's camp will cause a headache. In order to be effective, her majesty needs additional support from other pieces. In his turn, Black transfers another attacking piece to the kingside, which is now the critical zone of the board.

12 ♕f5+ ♔g7 13 ♔h1

Black has absolutely no problems after 13 ♗xg5 ♘xf3+ 14 ♕xf3 ♕xg5+ 15 ♔h1 ♔h8.

13...♔h8

Safety first! Both sides have put their kings on corner squares, where they will be harder to attack.

14 ♖g1 g4!

Black's queen impatiently desires to join the attack via the h4-square, and now the obstacle has been removed.

15 f4

Reiner desperately tries to keep lines closed, since Black's forces, one after another, are joining the assault.

15...♘f3 16 ♖xg4?!

But this capture is certainly contrary to the aim of keeping the position closed. Steinitz now concludes the game with some elegant sacrifices.

16...♕h4!! *(D)*

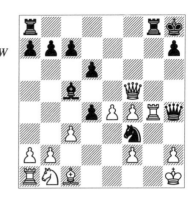

The queen is taboo: 17 ♖xh4 ♖g1#!

17 ♖g2

One last effort, but it's already much too late for salvation.

17...♕xh2+! 18 ♖xh2 ♖g1# (0-1)

This mating theme with rook and knight, called the *Arabian Mate*, is an instructive mechanism which chess-players of all levels should know by heart.

Bishop or Queen? It Depends...

Game 5
Knorre – Chigorin
St Petersburg 1874
Giuoco Piano

1 e4 e5 2 ♘f3 ♘c6 3 ♗c4 ♗c5 *(D)*

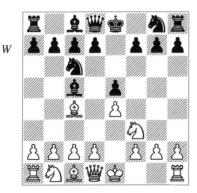

This is the *Giuoco Piano*. With this old but ever-popular opening, both sides aim to generate pressure on the f2/f7-squares. White in particular also has ideas of building a strong pawn-centre (with c3 and d4), while Black should be alert to chances to strike back with a well-timed ...d5 advance. However, the game can go in many different directions depending on the decisions taken by both sides.

4 0-0 ♘f6 5 d3 d6 6 ♗g5

Nowadays it is more popular to take a step towards forming a strong structure in the centre with 6 c3. The development of the bishop to g5, if employed at all, is generally delayed until Black has castled.

The most aggressive reaction to the text-move – ...h6 followed by ...g5 – now will not expose the black king to danger; this is why White generally waits for Black to castle. Chigorin illustrates these points in unforgettable style.

6...h6 7 ♗h4 g5

If Black had already played ...0-0, then this thrust could be met with a very dangerous ♘xg5 sacrifice. But now, the black king would not face any problems in that case.

8 ♗g3 *(D)*

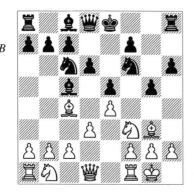

The stable centre (White is at least two moves from being able to make any sort of central pawn-break) encourages Black's following move, which launches a kingside attack. Black's uncastled king will remain fairly safe as long as the position remains relatively closed. It is a well-known principle that flank attacks are only likely to succeed if the centre is closed. Nevertheless, it is really hard to believe that Black's idea is so powerful.

8...h5!?

With the threat of trapping the bishop by ...h4. But isn't the g5-pawn *en prise*?

9 ♘xg5?!

9 h4 is a better idea.

9...h4 10 ♘xf7 *(D)*

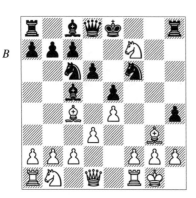

What is going on? Isn't it likely that the fork on f7 is much more important than trapping

the bishop? Sometimes we run into extraordinary positions in which pure concrete analysis of the variations (calculation) outweighs all other considerations. This position is certainly one of them...

10...hxg3!?

Chigorin gives up his queen too! It is quite understandable that Black doesn't want to lose his initiative. Still, it is rare for a mating attack to achieve success without the presence and support of a queen. Now, Black's main trump in the position is the half-open h-file.

It should be mentioned that 10...♛e7! is an excellent alternative that gives Black some advantage at least.

11 ♘xd8 *(D)*

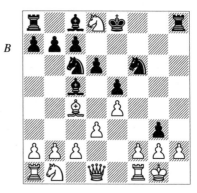

11...♗g4!

Developing with tempo is very important if Black is to deploy his forces around his opponent's king swiftly enough to justify his queen sacrifice.

12 ♛d2 *(D)*

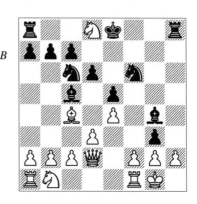

12...♘d4!

Material down, Black directs almost all of his remaining forces to the kingside. Now the simple but deadly threat is ...♘e2+ followed by ...♖xh2#. But shouldn't it be easy to repel this attack?

13 ♘c3?

White prevents the ...♘e2+ idea, but this is far from sufficient to save his skin. He needed to dig deeper and understand the true nature of Black's threats. Then he might have found the only way to avoid immediate loss: 13 h3 ♘e2+ (but not 13...♘f3+?? 14 gxf3 ♗xf3 15 ♕g5) 14 ♕xe2 ♗xe2 15 ♘e6 ♗b6 16 ♘c3 ♗xf1 17 ♔xf1 gxf2 18 ♘a4, with good chances of surviving.

13...♘f3+! (D)

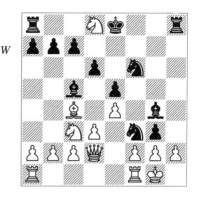

14 gxf3 ♗xf3 0-1

White is helpless against the mating threat ...gxh2#.

Potential in a Cramped Position

Game 6
Colburn – Blackburne
Hastings 1892
Centre Game

1 e4 e5 2 d4

By the end of the 19th century, it seems that the *Centre Game* still had loyal adherents, despite Steinitz's teachings regarding positional play. In this opening, White is not worried about the fact that his prematurely-developed queen is going to be harassed by ...♘c6. As White plans to castle queenside and attack his opponent on the kingside, he has to move his queen sooner or later.

2...exd4 3 ♕xd4 ♘c6 4 ♕e3

The queen temporarily blocks the diagonal of the dark-squared bishop. But Colburn, as we shall see, plans to transfer his queen to the kingside (g3 or h3) via the 3rd rank.

4...g6 (D)

Black foresees his opponent's plan of castling queenside, and therefore decides to fianchetto his bishop. Nowadays it is more common for Black to play more directly in the centre against the Centre Game: 4...♘f6 5 ♘c3 (5 e5?! ♘g4 6 ♕e4 d5!? 7 exd6+ ♗e6 gives Black a comfortable game) 5...♗b4 6 ♗d2 0-0 7 0-0-0 ♖e8 with mutual chances.

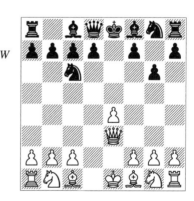

5 ♗d2 ♗g7 6 ♘c3 ♘ge7 7 0-0-0 0-0

These last few moves were all quite natural. Now White needs to concentrate on his desired kingside attack without allowing Black any counterplay. But his next move is suspicious and gives Black chances of active play.

8 f4?! (D)

At first glance, the advance of the pawn seems natural too, but White is underestimating Black's own active possibilities. After all, he has already castled and now his king is also safe. Blackburne seizes the initiative directly with a counter-blow in the centre, before White's dreamed-of attack has even started!

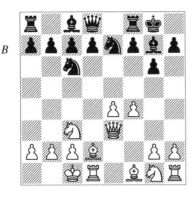

8...d5!

This outstanding move reveals the potential in Black's position. First of all, the simple threat is ...d4, winning a piece. But much more importantly, almost all the black forces (in particular the c8-bishop) will now support the attack against the enemy king, once White's domination of the centre is ended.

9 exd5 ♘b4! *(D)*

Black is not in a hurry to regain the pawn. Once again, the initiative is more important than material considerations.

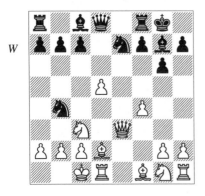

10 ♗c4 ♗f5!

After a series of forced moves, Black takes the lead in development. On the other hand, White has not managed to proceed even a bit with his kingside attack.

11 ♗b3 ♘exd5 12 ♘xd5 ♘xd5 13 ♕f3?! *(D)*

Although White makes seemingly natural moves, he cannot avoid falling into a bad position. In a chess game, you can always find

subtleties even in the simplest positions, if you analyse concretely. In this case, Black's fianchettoed bishop has sharply set its eyes on White's queenside. Unfortunately, Colburn doesn't pay attention to this important element and puts his queen on an irrelevant square (13 ♕c5 is relatively best, though Black still has excellent chances). As a result, he finds himself in a dead lost position.

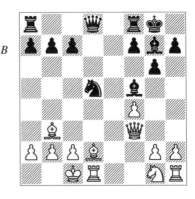

13...♕f6!

A simple yet very strong idea. To neutralize the pressure on b2, White now has to play 14 c3. But this advance increases the effect of the other bishop on f5.

14 c3 *(D)*

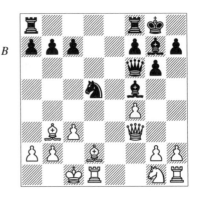

14...♘b4!

14 c3 has another negative effect: White's control over the d3-square is now significantly weakened. Blackburne tries to benefit from this 'hole', and his knight is taboo. Every pawn move gives up control of some squares, and since they don't move backwards, it's best to pay great attention to them.

15 ♗c4 *(D)*

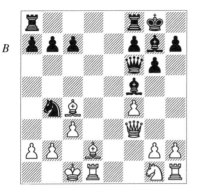

If we stop for a moment and look at the general picture, we see that almost all the action is taking place on the queenside, Black's main 'playground'. In a race to attack with opposite-side castling, this is a very bad sign for White.

White tries to stop ...♘d3+ with his move. But he fails to stop the following decisive series of moves.

15...♕a6!!

The queen craftily targets the king with the aid of the 'overloading' theme. Her majesty is immune: 16 ♗xa6? ♘xa2#.

16 g4 ♕xa2! 17 ♗e3

Desperately trying to open up a flight-square for the king on d2.

17...♗xc3!

No mercy!

0-1

The Tarrasch Trap

Game 7

Tarrasch – Marco

Dresden 1892

Ruy Lopez

1 e4 e5 2 ♘f3 ♘c6 3 ♗b5 d6 *(D)*

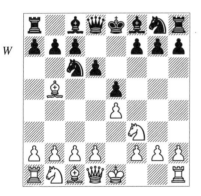

This move constitutes the *Steinitz Defence*. With his opening choice, Black aims to achieve a solid position. The risk is that it will be not only solid, but also passive. Nowadays this line is rare as White can set up rather strong pressure on e5, and other variations in the Ruy Lopez, such as the Berlin, Marshall, Chigorin and Breyer, etc., are seen more often.

4 d4

When our opponent does not stake a strong claim for the centre, then we have to take a step forward, if we wish to claim an edge. Siegbert Tarrasch, who was known as *Praeceptor Germaniae* ('Teacher of Germany'), declares his intentions with this move.

4...♗d7

Some decisions give a positional or a tactical shape to the upcoming struggle. By unpinning the knight and benefiting from the fact that the e4-pawn is also loose, Marco wants to protect his e5-pawn indirectly. Indeed after 5 ♗xc6 ♗xc6 6 dxe5?! dxe5 7 ♕xd8+?! ♖xd8 8 ♘xe5 ♗xe4, we certainly cannot talk about any kind of advantage for White. But the real question is for how long Black can withstand the pressure against e5.

5 ♘c3 ♘f6

Both sides continue to develop their pieces with the e4-pawn in mind.

6 0-0 ♗e7 7 ♖e1 0-0?

We reach the critical position, after the opening phase is more or less completed. White believes that he can win a pawn, now that he has solidly covered e4. But apparently Marco doesn't think so, as he feels that White will also have problems on his back rank. The only way to resolve this disagreement is through precise calculation. Trusting his own analysis, Tarrasch initiates a forcing sequence of moves, which will last almost to the end of the game.

8 ♗xc6

The first step against the e5-pawn: the guardian on c6 has now been removed.

8...♗xc6 *(D)*

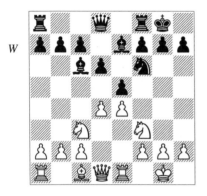

9 dxe5 dxe5 10 ♕xd8 ♖axd8 11 ♘xe5

Up to this point, the course of the game has been developing as expected. Now the question is whether Black can grab the pawn on e4.

11...♗xe4 12 ♘xe4 ♘xe4 13 ♘d3! *(D)*

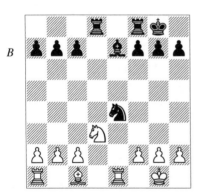

Thanks to this strong move, Tarrasch's idea can be seen more clearly: while blocking the black rook's path to the d1-square, White skewers Black's pieces on the adjacent file. At least for the moment, Marco still has some resources to keep him in the game.

13...f5

Only way to avoid material loss.

14 f3 ♗c5+

That's good news for Black: his bishop leaves the e-file with tempo. But c5 is also not the ideal square for the bishop...

15 ♘xc5 ♘xc5 16 ♗g5! *(D)*

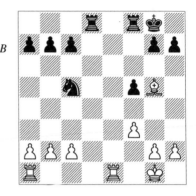

Now, Black's problem can be felt even more strongly: not only does the g5-bishop attack Black's rook, but at the same time a dangerous fork (♗e7) has arisen.

16...♖d5

Marco seeks salvation by protecting his vulnerable knight.

17 ♗e7 ♖e8 *(D)*

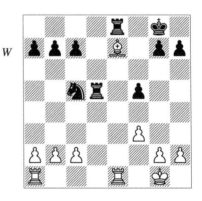

Finally, we reach the end of the series of forced moves that started on the 8th move.

18 c4! 1-0

The game is decided at once, as the coordination between Black's clumsy pieces is destroyed with this simple pawn advance. Black resigned as it is impossible to avoid material loss.

The series of forced moves that we witnessed in this game is known as the *Tarrasch*

Trap, and it has claimed quite a number of victims over the years.

Square-Clearance
Game 8
Steinitz – Von Bardeleben
Hastings 1895
Giuoco Piano

1 e4 e5 2 ♘f3 ♘c6 3 ♗c4 ♗c5 4 c3 *(D)*

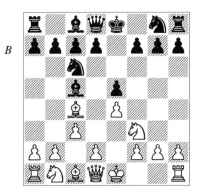

This game is another slugfest in the *Giuoco Piano*. As previously mentioned, White primarily tries to build a strong pawn-centre. 5 d4 is the intended follow-up, as 4 c3 has prepared to answer ...exd4 by recapturing with the c3-pawn. The Giuoco Piano is an ancient opening, and over the centuries some of its variations have been analysed as far as the endgame (or else to mate or perpetual check, etc.).

4...♘f6 5 d4 exd4 6 cxd4 ♗b4+

The tempo-gain from this check is vital, since other moves by the bishop would allow the white pawns to expand freely, sweeping everything from their path.

7 ♘c3!? *(D)*

An alternative variation, 7 ♗d2 ♗xd2+ 8 ♘bxd2 d5! 9 exd5 ♘xd5, results in an isolated queen's pawn (IQP) structure. In that case, White would try to claim an edge without sacrificing material (e.g., Game 36).

But in this game, Steinitz doesn't hesitate to give up his e-pawn in order to take a commanding lead in development.

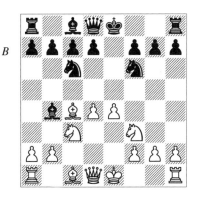

7...d5?

But this is a significant mistake from Von Bardeleben. With all his trumps, White is better prepared for the opening of the position. According to modern theory, 7...♘xe4 8 0-0 ♗xc3 9 d5 ♗f6 (9...♘e5 is also possible) 10 ♖e1 ♘e7 11 ♖xe4 d6 12 ♗g5 is fully satisfactory for Black.

8 exd5 ♘xd5 9 0-0 ♗e6

With the aim of reinforcing the knight and closing the e-file. But White can continue to develop his pieces with tempo.

10 ♗g5 ♗e7

The bishop has accomplished its mission on b4, and now heads back to e7 to take part in the defence. The tension between the pieces leads to the position opening up before Black has had time to castle. The critical matter for White is to decide which pieces to exchange and in what order. Steinitz duly chooses the most accurate series of moves.

11 ♗xd5!

First, let me point out that capturing the bishop with 11 ♗xe7?! would not give White anything after 11...♘cxe7, as it helps Black increase his control over d5. But now, it will be a stiffer test for the queen to preserve her influence over d5 and e7 simultaneously. This is the main reason for White to remove the knight first. After the exchanges, the black king will have to remain in the centre.

11...♗xd5 *(D)*

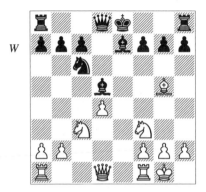

12 ♘xd5 ♕xd5 13 ♗xe7 ♘xe7 14 ♖e1

The sequence of exchanges has ended. In general, in isolated queen's pawn (IQP) structures, exchanges usually favour the side playing against the IQP. But in this specific position, the king's obligation to keep an eye on the knight is the main reason for Black's problems.

14...f6 *(D)*

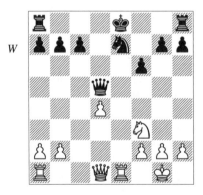

A useful move: Black aims to escape his opponent's pressure along the e-file by playing ...♔f7. At the same time, he limits the f3-knight's mobility by seizing control over e5 and g5.

15 ♕e2

It seems logical to step up the pressure on the e-file. But here, some analysis from masters

shows that White had another effective move at his disposal: 15 ♕a4+!. The idea behind this crafty move is to sustain the initiative after 15...c6 16 ♕a3 or 15...♔f7 16 ♘e5+!.

15...♕d7 16 ♖ac1 c6?

Black seeks to prevent the ever-present danger of White making the d5 advance. But Black should have given priority to evacuating his king from the e-file, and so connect his rooks.

17 d5! *(D)*

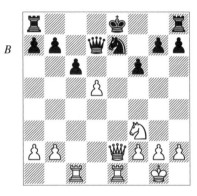

An excellent move with a *square-clearance* theme. Now, the d4-square is opened for the knight's use. As Black's queen and knight are bound hand and foot, White's menacing pawn must be removed by the c-pawn.

17...cxd5 18 ♘d4

Thus, the previously ineffective knight now turns into one of the most powerful weapons in White's army.

18...♔f7 19 ♘e6 ♖hc8

White's rook was threatening to penetrate Black's camp with ♖c7. But now the queen finds a devastating way to join the attack.

20 ♕g4!

In addition to the obvious threat of ♕xg7+, White threatens to exploit the black queen's loose position with ♘g5+.

20...g6 21 ♘g5+ ♔e8

The black king has no choice but to return to its initial square; otherwise, the queen would hang on d7.

22 ♖xe7+! *(D)*

The queen has set her sights (via the *X-ray* theme!) on the c8-rook, and this fact is the foundation of Steinitz's unbelievable sacrifice: 22...♕xe7 23 ♖xc8+ ♖xc8 24 ♕xc8+ ♕d8 25

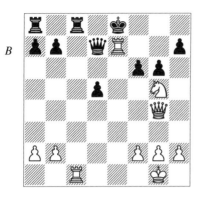

B

♕xd8+ ♚xd8 and White heads to the endgame with a knight advantage. The other alternative, 22...♚xe7, would obviously fail as well: 23 ♖e1+ ♚d6 24 ♕b4+ ♖c5 25 ♖e6+ and White wins.

Instead, Von Bardeleben comes up with a nice idea to benefit from his opponent's apparently weak back rank:

22...♚f8!

Black's queen cannot be taken as suddenly the ...♖xc1+ idea emerges.

23 ♖f7+!

What a game! Now it's Steinitz's turn to prove that his rook is invulnerable! Once again, we see White keep an extra piece after 23...♕xf7 24 ♖xc8+.

23...♚g8!

A real game of cat and mouse. But White is also persistent in his claim.

24 ♖g7+! ♚h8

Trying to revert with 24...♚f8 would fail to 25 ♘xh7+ ♚xg7 (25...♚e8 26 ♘xf6+ and White wins) 26 ♕xd7+.

25 ♖xh7+!

The 'fugitive' is now caught, as with the h-file's clearance, the queen finds an additional line for her usage: 25...♚g8 26 ♖g7+ ♚h8 27 ♕h4+! ♚xg7 28 ♕h7+ ♚f8 29 ♕h8+ ♚e7 30 ♕g7+ ♚e8 31 ♕g8+ ♚e7 32 ♕f7+ ♚d8 33 ♕f8+ ♕e8 34 ♘f7+ (finally!) 34...♚d7 35 ♕d6#.

1-0

A real gem of a game from one of the greatest players of the late 19th century!

Pawn-Grabbing in the Opening

Game 9

Mieses – Chigorin

Ostend 1906

Vienna Game

1 e4 e5 2 ♘c3 *(D)*

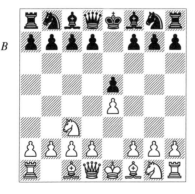

B

The *Vienna Game*. While this is fundamentally a simple developing move, it can also herald an aggressive approach in the opening. That is because White's f-pawn is still free to advance, and this can lead to play similar to the King's Gambit. Rather than play it as a gambit, White might also make the f4 advance after further preparation, seeking to utilize a half-open f-file or to make a general advance on the kingside. There are also other ways to seek to profit from the fact that White has not played ♘f3, as we shall see in the game.

2...♘c6 3 ♗c4 ♗c5 4 ♕g4

Mieses seeks to sow disorder in Black's position by attacking the g7-pawn, which became vulnerable after the f8-bishop's development.

4...♕f6?

This move looks ideal at a glance: Black protects the g7-pawn, while also counterattacking White's f2-pawn. But we must always bear in mind that just because we have made a threat, it isn't compulsory for the opponent to prevent it. For what *is* Black's threat, in fact? ...♕xf2+ is not mate, but just a check. If Chigorin had weighed his decision more carefully, he would perhaps have realized that White had a strong reply that makes great gains at the cost of this mere pawn.

The standard moves are 4...♔f8 and 4...g6.

5 ♘d5! *(D)*

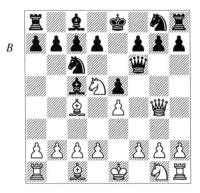

In just a couple of moves, the calm character of the battle has suddenly transformed into a sharp fight. Far from being reluctant to give up his f2-pawn, Mieses willingly sacrifices it! Exposing our own king with such an idea seems risky, doesn't it? But actually, it is the black queen and king that are truly exposed, while Black is falling behind in development.

5...♕xf2+

The bishop would drop off after 5...♗xf2+? 6 ♔f1.

6 ♔d1 ♔f8

Defending g7, while escaping from White's knight fork on c7.

7 ♘h3!

The first instance of development with tempo. Once again, Black has to move his queen.

7...♕d4?!

It is better to insert 7...h5 8 ♕g5 before playing 8...♕d4, as then 9 d3 ♗e7 leaves Black with more defensive chances, though White retains a substantial advantage.

8 d3

Suddenly there appears the idea of trapping the queen with c3.

8...d6 *(D)*

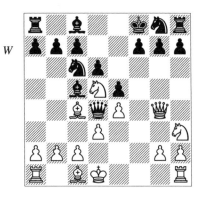

9 ♕h4

It appears like Mieses does not trust his chances of 'mating' the queen, because he mostly focuses on his attack against the king. Nevertheless, a plan with 9 ♕g3 might discomfort Black's queen in many possible variations. For example, 9...♗xh3 10 ♖f1! ♗b6 11 c3 ♕c5 12 b4 and Black has to accept big material losses in order to save his queen.

9...♗xh3 10 ♕xh3 ♘a5?

But now, Black had to parry his opponent's main threat, ♖f1, by playing 10...♕f2. Even so, the principal problem in his position is once again his queen, and White can prove his advantage as follows: 11 ♗d2! (threatening ♗e1, followed by c3) 11...♘d4 12 ♘xc7 (or immediately 12 c3) 12...♖d8 13 c3! (freeing c2 for the king's use, and at the same time allowing the rook to join the fight) 13...♘c6 14 ♔c2! and White wins. When one sees such complicated variations, we may conclude that while sacrifices are usually motivated by general considerations, they are justified by precise calculation.

11 ♖f1!

After taking control over f2, the c3 advance becomes a concrete threat. Also, serious attacking chances will emerge along the f-file.

11...♘xc4 12 ♕d7! *(D)*

It is too early for White to relax. For a few moves, the c3 advance has been one of White's main resources, but here, this move would ruin the position: 12 c3? ♘xb2+! 13 ♗xb2 ♕a4+ and suddenly the game is very far from clear.

Thus it is time for White to refocus his attack squarely on the black king. With each move, the position on the board changes, and so can the best plans for both sides.

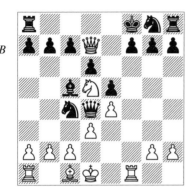

12...f6 13 ᐁxf6!
Destroying the king's position. Creating similar threats with 13 ♗h6! is also an elegant and effective option.
13...♕f2

Desperately trying to prolong the game. The knight was taboo: 13...ᐁxf6 14 ♖xf6+! gxf6 15 ♗h6+ ♔g8 16 ♕g7#.
14 ♖xf2 ♗xf2 15 ᐁh5 *(D)*

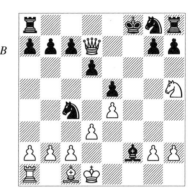

1-0
The attack on g7 could only be stopped temporarily with 15...ᐁe7; after 16 ♗g5 ♖e8 17 dxc4 White has a decisive material plus and he still retains his attacking chances.

Rubinstein's Heritage
Game 10
Rotlewi – Rubinstein
Lodz 1907/8
Symmetrical Tarrasch

1 d4 d5 2 ᐁf3 e6 3 e3 c5 4 c4 *(D)*

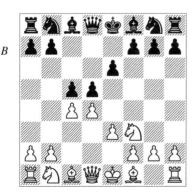

This game is heading towards a symmetrical form of the *Tarrasch Defence* to the *Queen's Gambit* (the pure Tarrasch is 1 d4 d5 2 c4 e6 3

ᐁc3 c5). It is hard for both sides to maintain the tension in the centre for too long without allowing the opponent a favourable way to make an exchange of pawns. So within a few moves the structure will become more stable.
4...ᐁc6 5 ᐁc3 ᐁf6 6 dxc5
Generally speaking, releasing the tension is in itself a concession; moreover, it helps Black develop in this particular position. Nevertheless, White plans to attack Black's bishop (which will come to c5) with pawn advances, and so gain time and space. It is not so easy to find an 'ideal' move, since after, e.g., 6 ♗d3, Black could reply 6...dxc4, when White will lose time with his bishop – in fact, after 7 ♗xc4 he has the same position that Black gets after his next move in our game.

6...♗xc5 7 a3 a6 8 b4

White expands on the queenside, while preparing his bishop's development.

8...♗d6 9 ♗b2 0-0 (D)

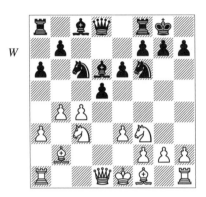

10 ♕d2

First of all, let's note that White can't win a pawn by capturing three times on d5, since White loses his queen after 10 cxd5 exd5 11 ♘xd5?? (11 ♗e2 is safe enough) 11...♘xd5 12 ♕xd5 ♗xb4+. For now, Rotlewi wants to keep his pressure against the d5-pawn, and he makes another useful waiting move before developing his bishop. But the queen is poorly placed on d2, and the right way to regroup is 10 ♕c2 followed by ♖d1.

10...♕e7!

This strong pawn sacrifice is based on the fact that White's king still stands in the centre. Of course, it is not obligatory for White to accept the offer. Nevertheless, to understand the logic behind Black's idea, we should analyse the capture: 11 cxd5 exd5 12 ♘xd5 ♘xd5 13 ♕xd5 ♘xb4!? (Black would also achieve an active position after 13...♖d8 14 ♕b3 a5 15 b5 ♘e5, but the piece sacrifice is far more ambitious) 14 axb4 ♗xb4+ 15 ♔e2 ♗d7. In addition to the white king's uncomfortable position, the bishop-pair's influence in this open position gives Black enough play. So as not to face this type of scenario, Rotlewi decides to continue with his development.

11 ♗d3?! dxc4

The right moment for the capture, because White now has to make a second move with his bishop.

12 ♗xc4 b5 13 ♗d3 ♖d8

Placing a rook on the same file as the enemy queen is often a good idea. White decides he has nothing better than losing a tempo, rather than facing some unpleasant tricks.

14 ♕e2 ♗b7 15 0-0 ♘e5 (D)

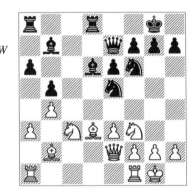

In this near-symmetrical position, White has lost so much time that it is Black who is seeking the initiative. But can't White gain some space with a pawn advance after exchanging on e5?

16 ♘xe5 ♗xe5 17 f4 ♗c7 18 e4

Rotlewi wants to prevent his opponent's idea of challenging the centre with ...e5: he would now meet 18...e5 with 19 f5. Still, these pawn advances lose control of some important squares in the heart of White's position. This might not matter so much if he could back up his pawns with active piece-play, but White is still behind in development. Also, repelling the bishop is no great achievement, since bishops are long-range pieces which retain their influence from afar.

18...♖ac8 19 e5?!

White has the perfectly reasonable idea of putting a piece on e4 and neutralizing the bishops' pressure by further exchanges. But there just isn't time, and this third pawn-push is way too much for White's fragile position to stand. Rubinstein is fully aware of the weak squares that these advances leave behind, and understands that he must act with the utmost vigour to prove his case. He finds a forcing path to a decisive advantage.

19...♗b6+

First of all, Black takes control over the a7-g1 diagonal.

20 ♔h1 (D)

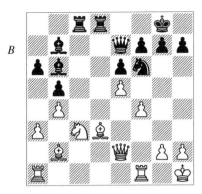

20...♞g4!

Can't White just take this knight? No, since after 21 ♛xg4 ♜xd3, the attack on White's own knight gives Black the initiative: 22 ♜ac1 ♜d2!. OK, but what is Black seeking to achieve with this knight move? He intends to bring his queen into the assault with devastating effect by ...♛h4. In addition, ...♞f2+ is a menace in many variations.

21 ♗e4

Rotlewi puts his idea of exchanges on the e4-square into practice. The main problem is that Black has far better options than dutifully trading pieces.

21...♛h4 22 g3 *(D)*

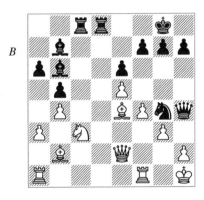

It was very important to cut off the queen's control over f2, while beating off the checkmate threat. Still, Black has an awesome trump in his hand!

22...♜xc3!

Overwhelming Rotlewi's queen, which has the task of defending the h2- and e4-squares simultaneously.

23 gxh4

White seeks salvation in sweeping away the queen, as it is mate after 23 ♗xc3 ♗xe4+ 24 ♛xe4 ♛xh2#.

23...♜d2!! *(D)*

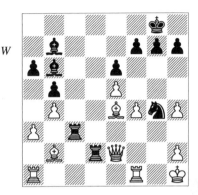

Another excellent move on the theme of *overload*.

24 ♛xd2

Whichever rook is taken, the result will be more or less the same: 24 ♗xc3 ♜xe2 (threatening ...♜xh2#) 25 ♜f2 ♗xe4+ 26 ♔g1 ♗xf2+ 27 ♔f1 ♗f3 (preparing the mate by protecting the rook on e2), followed by ...♞xh2#.

24...♗xe4+ 25 ♛g2 ♜h3!! *(D)*

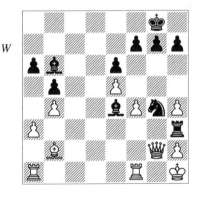

0-1

This is Rubinstein's most famous game and can deservedly be called a masterpiece. 106 years passed. Then World Champion Anand won a marvellous game against Aronian in the 2013 Wijk aan Zee tournament. In the postmortem, Vishy Anand mentioned that many ideas in his victory somewhat resembled Rubinstein's classic game. Let's see if you agree with him...

A Similar Game:

Aronian – Anand
Wijk aan Zee 2013
Semi-Slav Defence

1 d4 d5 2 c4 c6 3 ♘f3 ♘f6 4 ♘c3 e6 5 e3 ♘bd7 6 ♗d3 dxc4

The *Meran Variation*. In this sharp system, Black gives up his post on d5 and prepares the ...b5 advance in order to solve the problem of developing his light-squared bishop while generating queenside counterplay. But this change in the character of the position also allows White to set up a pawn-centre with the e4 advance. The battle between attacks on the flank and in the centre creates a very rich game.

7 ♗xc4 b5 8 ♗d3 ♗d6 9 0-0 0-0 10 ♕c2 ♗b7 11 a3

First of all, White wants to prevent the ...b4 advance. At the same time, he prepares his own b4 advance, so as to stop the freeing move ...c5.

11...♖c8 *(D)*

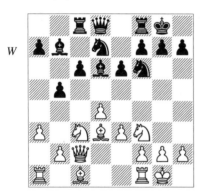

12 ♘g5

The continuation of the above-mentioned plan, 12 b4, leads to a sharp fight after 12...a5 (even 12...c5 is possible!) 13 ♖b1 axb4 14 axb4 ♕e7, etc.

Instead, Aronian is ready to sacrifice his h2-pawn, hoping to gain attacking chances in return.

12...c5

12...♗xh2+ 13 ♔xh2 ♘g4+ 14 ♔g1 ♕xg5 15 f3 ♘gf6 16 e4 would create a truly unbalanced position. But Anand doesn't want to allow his opponent to seize the initiative by accepting White's gift. He doesn't hesitate to sacrifice his own pawn to activate the b7-bishop.

13 ♘xh7

13 ♗xh7+ has been tried in some later games, without a final verdict being reached.

13...♘g4

The first step: the knight joins the fray, as in the Rotlewi-Rubinstein game...

14 f4 cxd4 15 exd4 *(D)*

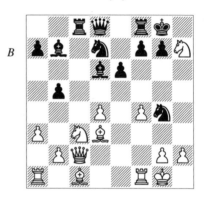

15...♗c5!

Black can sacrifice this bishop, since after 16 dxc5 ♘xc5, the bishop cannot retreat to safety with 17 ♗e2?, as 17...♕d4+ is a devastating reply.

16 ♗e2 ♘de5!! *(D)*

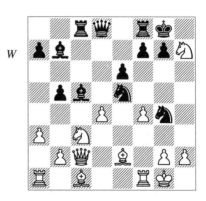

Unbelievable: the bishop and knight fork themselves. Black's pressure on d4 outweighs all other considerations.

17 ♗xg4

In his analysis, Anand gave this nice variation: 17 fxe5 ♕xd4+ 18 ♔h1 ♕g1+! 19 ♖xg1 ♘f2# and *smothered mate*! Aronian decides to remove the knight first. But in a couple of moves, the other knight will also join the attack from precisely this square.

17...♗xd4+ 18 ♔h1 ♘xg4 19 ♘xf8 *(D)*

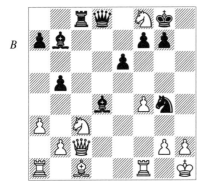

19...f5!

There's no need to hurry to capture the knight. Anand's deadly threat is now ...♕h4. The immediate 19...♕h4 would result in an exchange of queens after 20 ♕h7+!.

20 ♘g6

Stopping the ...♕h4 idea, but this defensive try only delays the inevitable: the queen will find a way in.

20...♕f6 21 h3

21 ♘e5 ♘xh2! would have been decisive.

21...♕xg6 22 ♕e2 ♕h5 *(D)*

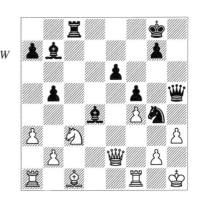

OK, so we don't have a pair of rook sacrifices in this game – it is the minor pieces that performed the fancy footwork. But the black bishops' powerful postures on the most critical diagonals very much resembles Rubinstein's immortal victory.

23 ♕d3

Trying to block the b7-bishop's diagonal with 23 ♖f3 would not make any significant difference to the outcome: 23...♘f2+ 24 ♔h2 (24 ♖xf2 ♕xh3+ 25 ♔g1 ♕xg2#) 24...♗xf3 25 ♕xf3 ♖xf3 26 gxf3 ♗xc3 27 bxc3 ♖xc3 and Black wins (Anand).

23...♗e3

Threatening ...♕xh3# with this interference theme is the finishing touch.

0-1

Knowing the classics by heart is always rewarding.

Undeveloped Queenside

Game 11

Roesch – Schlage

Hamburg 1910

Ruy Lopez

1 e4 e5 2 ♘f3 ♘c6 3 ♗b5 a6 4 ♗a4 ♘f6 5 ♕e2 *(D)*

With this move, known as the *Wormald Attack*, White doesn't want to allow his opponent to capture his e-pawn with ...♘xe4. The closely related *Worrall Attack* features 5 0-0 ♗e7 6 ♕e2 (rather than the standard 6 ♖e1), but that move-order gives Black the option of meeting 5 0-0 with 5...♘xe4, leading to the Open Defence.

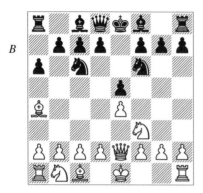

5...b5 6 ♗b3 ♗e7 7 c3 0-0 8 0-0 d5!? *(D)*

With this aggressive move, Black is willing to give up a pawn in order to seize the initiative. This idea is similar to the Marshall Attack, in which Black makes the same move but with the white queen on d1 and the rook on e1 (i.e. 5 0-0 ♗e7 6 ♖e1 b5 7 ♗b3 0-0 8 c3 d5!?).

Black can also play the more solid 8...d6, protecting the e5-pawn. He can follow up by challenging the 'Lopez bishop' with a timely ...♘a5. For example, 9 ♖d1 ♘a5 10 ♗c2 c5 11 d4 ♕c7 and apart from the locations of White's queen and rook, we have the same position as in *Chigorin Variation*.

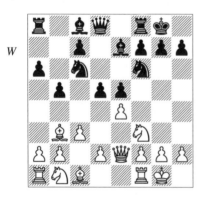

Schlage's combative choice seeks a sharp game.

9 exd5

Given that White can't easily digest the e5-pawn (as the game continuation demonstrates), nowadays this capture is viewed as a premature opening of the centre that eases Black's development. Schlage grounds his plan on White's undeveloped queenside, as well as his own easy and active play. Therefore, keeping the tension

with 9 d3 is much more popular. This modest move leads to a manoeuvring game in a closed position.

9...♘xd5 10 ♘xe5 *(D)*

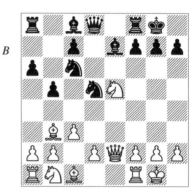

10...♘f4

Black's pawn sacrifice is based on time-gaining, aggressive moves like this. The knight that has just landed on f4 is a powerful weapon on its own. The weakness of d3 is also clearly visible.

11 ♕e4 ♘xe5!!

A great assessment: Black is well aware of the fact that his knight's participation in the assault is much more valuable than the rook in the corner.

12 ♕xa8??

Rejecting the exchange sacrifice with 12 ♕xe5?? does not help White either: 12...♗d6! (these forcing moves do not allow White's queenside pieces to join the game) 13 ♕e4 ♕h4! and it is impossible to resist Black's well-conducted attack.

12 ♕xf4?! ♘d3 gives Black a firm grip on the game, but isn't an instant catastrophe for White. The only good move is 12 d4, when 12...♗b7 13 ♕xb7 ♘e2+ 14 ♔h1 ♘xc1 15 ♖xc1 ♘d3 is OK for Black.

12...♕d3!!

Not allowing White to play d4! Now White is faced with several dangerous threats simultaneously. Certainly, the most important one is 13...♘e2+ 14 ♔h1 ♘g3+! 15 hxg3 (15 fxg3 ♕xf1#) 15...♕xf1+ 16 ♔h2 ♘g4+ 17 ♔h3 ♕h1#. Therefore, White parries this threat, but alas it is far from Black's only idea.

13 ♗d1 ♗h3! *(D)*

Black's forces pile into the kingside one after another. Moreover, the bishop discovers an attack on the white queen.

Black actually had a very pleasant choice here, with 13...♘h3+! 14 gxh3 ♗xh3 one of several other winning lines.

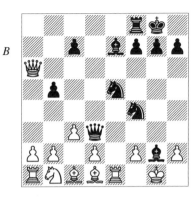

It's quite remarkable to witness that nearly all of White's pieces are lined up on his first rank, whereas Black's forces are a picture of activity.

15...♛f3!

A flamboyant queen sacrifice. White is helpless against ...♘h3#.

0-1

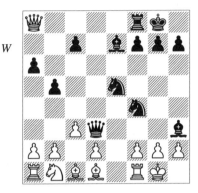

14 ♛xa6 ♗xg2 15 ♖e1 *(D)*

Just Like a Magnet...

Game 12
Ed. Lasker – Thomas
London (casual game) 1912
Dutch Defence

1 d4 e6 2 ♘f3 f5 *(D)*

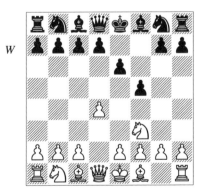

A typical *Dutch Defence* (1 d4 f5) position, although reached from a different move-order. Both sides have a variety of trumps in this asymmetrical opening. In a few moves, however, our present game will revolve around the e4-square. White will try to seize control of this important post, while Black will do his best to avoid this happening.

3 ♘c3 ♘f6

After seeing the notes above, one may wonder why Thomas did not choose 3...d5, which would duly strengthen Black's control over e4. It is a perfectly playable option, of course, but the perennially weak e5-square and problems with the c8-bishop are not to everyone's taste.

4 ♗g5 ♗e7

Black unpins his knight, so that he will at least gain the bishop-pair in return for losing his potential outpost on e4.

5 ♗xf6 ♗xf6 6 e4 fxe4 7 ♘xe4 b6 8 ♘e5

Moving the knight for the second time, before even touching the f1-bishop, is quite unusual. White wants to create threats (such as ♛h5+) by placing his knights close to Black's camp.

8...0-0 *(D)*

Thomas declines to capture the knight at once, as surrendering the dark-squared bishop may leave him with a weak colour-complex: 8...♗xe5 9 ♕h5+ g6 10 ♕xe5 0-0 11 c3. Most of the time, castling is in accordance with the motto '*safety first*'.

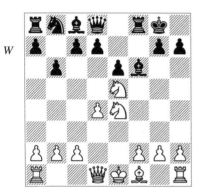

9 ♗d3?! ♗b7?!

Now, however, 9...♗xe5 10 dxe5 ♘c6 is surprisingly awkward for White to answer.

10 ♕h5 ♕e7?? *(D)*

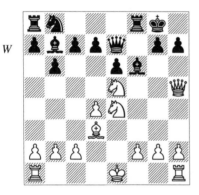

In a chess battle, our opponent's thoughts are just as important as our own ideas, but Black appears to have forgotten this. Understanding the changes caused by the opponent's last move must be a basic part of our decision-making process.

For the first nine moves of the game, both sides had been improving their positions in a more or less normal manner, developing pieces and controlling squares, etc. But White's tenth move brought his queen and bishop to bear on h7 – but for the presence of the knight on e4, he

would be threatening mate in one. This means that there is a powerful *battery* on the b1-h7 diagonal. While Black's last move parries the most direct threat – i.e. 11 ♘xf6+ followed by taking on h7 – with so much firepower aligned against the black king, it should be no surprise that White has other powerful attacking ideas. Figuring out precisely what those ideas are, however, requires considerable ingenuity and accurate calculation.

11 ♕xh7+!!

This shocking queen sacrifice needed to be precisely worked out. Now Black is helpless against the constant threats from White's minor pieces. Just like a magnet, White's forces will pull the black king right into White's own camp.

11...♔xh7 12 ♘xf6++ ♔h6 *(D)*

12...♔h8? 13 ♘g6# would be immediately terminal.

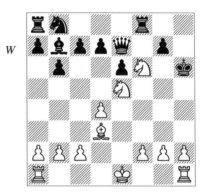

13 ♘eg4+!

When a queen is sacrificed, it is essential to calculate all the complicated variations right to the end, and foresee the final position clearly. After all, if Black could somehow save his king even at a considerable material cost, then White might end up losing. The hardest part of White's sacrificial plan was to decide with which knight to check on the 13th move. 13 ♘fg4+? would not yield White a winning advantage, since this knight's control over h5 is still very important: 13...♔h5! (13...♔g5? 14 h4+ ♔f4 15 g3#) 14 ♗g6+ ♔h4 15 g3+ ♔h3 and it is not possible to talk about a checkmate.

How do we develop the ability to calculate long sequences accurately? One way is by solving many tactical exercises, starting with easy ones before moving on to ones that require greater degrees of calculation and vision.

13...♔g5 14 h4+ ♔f4

From now on, it is quite easy to predict that Black's king will be 'captured' very soon.

15 g3+ ♔f3 16 ♗e2+

16 0-0, followed by ♘h2#, would lead to checkmate in one move less, but the text-move is more than sufficient.

16...♔g2 17 ♖h2+ ♔g1 18 ♔d2# *(D)* **(1-0)**

The final position rightfully deserves a diagram.

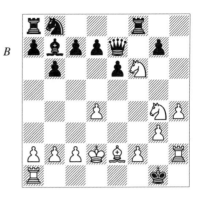

When the f-Pawn Marches...

Game 13
Opočensky – Hrdina
Mlada Boleslav 1913
Four Knights Game

1 e4 e5 2 ♘f3 ♘c6 3 ♘c3 ♘f6 *(D)*

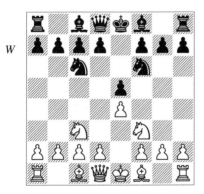

This is the appropriately-named *Four Knights Game*. The seemingly-quiet character of this ancient opening can be misleading: Black cannot maintain the symmetry indefinitely, and the extra half-move that White possesses can prove vitally important. That said, this is a well-explored opening system where Black has a variety of viable options.

4 ♗b5

Opočensky simply proceeds with his development. Taking action in the centre with 4 d4 is the main alternative, generally leading to the 'Scotch Four Knights' after 4...exd4 5 ♘xd4. But continuing in 'Italian Game fashion' with 4 ♗c4?! would be answered by tactical means: 4...♘xe4, based on the pawn fork 5 ♘xe4 d5.

4...♗b4 5 0-0 0-0 6 d3 d6 7 ♗g5 ♘e7!? *(D)*

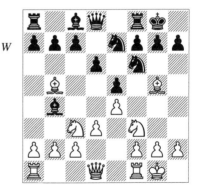

A curious decision: Black allows his opponent to ruin his structure on the kingside. With the knight retreat, he's aiming to challenge the now rather lost-looking b5-bishop with ...c6 and then proceed with ...d5, taking the initiative in the centre. Nevertheless, Opočensky declines the opportunity to play ♗xf6. Maybe he felt that after 8 ♗xf6 gxf6, Black's potential play on the g-file and/or with an ...f5 advance at some point would prove more important than the weakening of Black's kingside structure.

8 ♘h4!?

Opening the way for both the f-pawn and the queen, while simultaneously parrying ideas of ...♘g6.

8...c6 9 ♗c4 ♘g6 *(D)*

Unprincipled play. As mentioned before, Black could make his voice heard in the centre with 9...d5; e.g., 10 ♗xf6 gxf6 11 ♗b3 f5. The text-move, however, justifies White's ♘h4 manoeuvre.

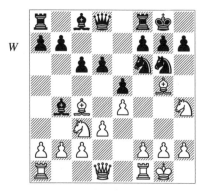

10 ♘xg6 hxg6 11 f4

On the other hand, White's play is truly consistent. Opening the f-file offers him attacking chances. But one should emphasize that Black is not yet deprived of counterplay either.

11...♕b6+ 12 ♔h1 ♘g4?! *(D)*

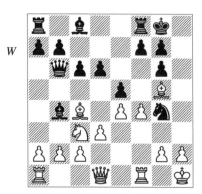

With his last couple of moves, Black has proved that the pin on f6 was not critical. But the real issue is whether the knight's journey into White's camp is justified.

13 ♕e1

It seems that 13 ♕f3! followed by ♖ae1 may be a more logical set-up. This also prevents 13...♘e3 since 14 ♘a4! would give White the advantage immediately.

The purpose of the text-move is to transfer the queen to the h-file as quickly as possible. Still, as Black has his own counterplay, the position is far from decided.

13...♘e3 14 f5! *(D)*

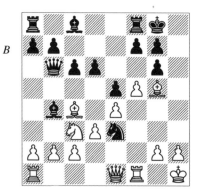

If you have said 'a', you must also say 'b'! Due to the light-squared bishop's influence over the a2-g8 diagonal, Black's threat of winning the exchange can now be ignored: attacking possibilities (first on g6, then h7) allow White to put this aggressive approach into practice.

14...♘xc4?

As 14...♘xf1? 15 fxg6 d5 16 ♕h4 fxg6 17 exd5 would be terminal, Hrdina decides to gobble the bishop. However, this also loses, and Black should have played 14...♗xc3, though 15 ♕xe3! will leave Black with an unpleasant endgame.

15 f6! *(D)*

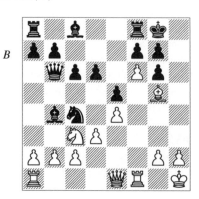

Black's light-square weaknesses have been somewhat remedied by the removal of White's light-squared bishop. Still, as checkmate foregoes every other consideration, White penetrates Black's camp via the dark squares despite the substantial cost in material. The switch from a light-squared attack to one on the dark squares is an elegant feature of the game.

15...♗g4

Desperately trying to close the h-file. But this attempt turns out to be rather slow, and as a result Black will fail in his defence.

16 ♕h4 ♗h5 17 g4

Breaking open the h-file.

17...♘e3 18 gxh5!

Just like we've witnessed with 15 f6!, there is no need to worry about material losses when mate is the goal: Opočensky is well aware that his attacking forces are more than enough to succeed.

18...♘xf1 19 h6 *(D)*

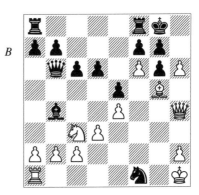

1-0

An elegant finale!

Improving the Pieces

Game 14
Capablanca – Fonaroff
New York 1918
Ruy Lopez

1 e4 e5 2 ♘f3 ♘c6 3 ♗b5 ♘f6

Nowadays, when Black plays 3...♘f6 against the Ruy Lopez, one usually assumes that he is aiming to reach the 'Berlin queenless middlegame' after 4 0-0 ♘xe4 5 d4 ♘d6 6 ♗xc6 dxc6 7 dxe5 ♘f5 8 ♕xd8+ ♔xd8, an opening line that has been tested in thousands of high-level games in the 21st century. But in the first quarter of the 20th century, it would be odd to claim that Black was aware of all the critical defensive techniques and nuances of that variation. In this game, Fonaroff puts a 'Steinitz' approach into practice with this next move.

4 0-0 d6

This pawn advance is Steinitz's main influence on Black's play. In this system there is a thin line between achieving a solid position and being left in a passive situation where White can freely develop his play in the centre. Black's main goal is to pursue solidity with an eye on securing active counterplay at the right moment.

5 d4

With Black staking little claim for the centre, it is fully appropriate for White to seek the initiative in this area of the board. Otherwise, Black might duly acquire his desired solid and comfortable position.

5...♗d7 6 ♘c3 ♗e7 7 ♖e1 *(D)*

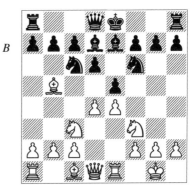

7...exd4

Immediately releasing the tension, but was it so urgent? After 7...a6 (for 7...0-0, see Game 7) 8 ♗xc6 ♗xc6 9 dxe5 dxe5 10 ♕xd8+ ♖xd8 11 ♘xe5 ♗xe4 12 ♘xe4 ♘xe4 13 ♗h6 (in order to open the way for the rook, but the simple 13 ♘d3 might give White more chances) 13...♘xf2 14 ♗xg7 ♖g8 15 ♔xf2 ♖xg7 16 ♘d3, it is not easy to talk about a significant advantage for White. Therefore we can question the timing of this exchange, which allows White's pieces to land strongly in the centre.

8 ♘xd4 ♘xd4 9 ♕xd4 ♗xb5 10 ♘xb5 0-0 (D)

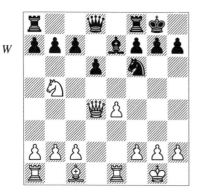

11 ♕c3

A tactical theme, *square-clearance*, is employed here for purely positional purposes. While attacking the c7-pawn, White is actually clearing the d4-square for the knight's use. This enables the knight, which is currently rather functionless on b5, to play a far more critical role on f5. Knights are short-range pieces, and so are most effective when close to the enemy camp.

11...c6?!

A tactical defence with 11...♕d7!? offers Black a more comfortable game: 12 ♘xc7? loses to 12...♖ac8, while after 12 ♕xc7 ♕xb5 13 ♕xe7 ♖fd8!, Black intends ...♖d7, harassing White's queen. 12 ♘d4 is of course a move to consider – after all, White's main goal was to improve the position of his knight. Then 12...d5! 13 e5 ♘e4 (this tempo is important; Black needs to gain some time for the ...c5 push) 14 ♕d3 c5! gives Black a perfectly reasonable position.

Of course, it is easy to criticize Black's play after seeing the result of the game. Fonaroff's

last move seems very logical: the threat against the pawn is parried with a counter-threat, and he prepares ...d5, which would question White's domination in the centre. Let's see if Capablanca's plan of transferring the knight to f5 will pass this test.

12 ♘d4 ♘d7

Black could stop the ♘f5 idea at once with 12...g6, but then White would have the upper hand, as he will swiftly complete his development with 13 ♗h6 followed by ♖ad1.

13 ♘f5 ♗f6 14 ♕g3 ♘e5 (D)

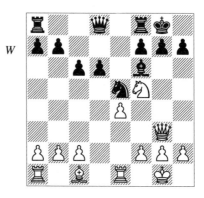

15 ♗f4!

This is much more effective than 15 f4, when Black could reply 15...♘g6 (with ...♘h4 ideas; 15...♘c4!? is also playable) 16 ♕d3 d5 17 e5 ♗e7. The mobile e- and f-pawns are dangerous weapons, but Black retains reasonable defensive prospects.

But after the text-move, Black feels very uncomfortable because of his d-pawn, which became quite vulnerable when Black played ...c6.

15...♕c7 16 ♖ad1 ♖ad8 (D)

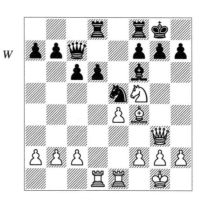

It is now time for White to go for an all-out attack, since he's placed all of his pieces in their ideal locations. The f5-knight's influence is felt particularly strongly. Now 17 h4!? is one tempting way to continue the attack, but Capablanca initiates immediate action.

17 ♖xd6 ♖xd6 18 ♗xe5 ♖d1?

This interesting yet unsuccessful attempt aims to benefit from White's back-rank problems. Fonaroff challenges his famous opponent to justify his play. He gets more than he bargained for!

18...♕a5! keeps Black in the game, by targeting the e1-rook. After 19 ♗c3 ♗xc3 20 bxc3 ♖g6 21 ♘e7+ ♔h8 22 ♘xg6+ hxg6 White has little or no advantage.

19 ♖xd1 ♗xe5 20 ♘h6+ ♔h8 *(D)*

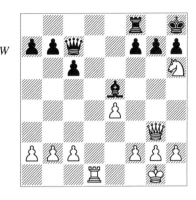

21 ♕xe5!

Another sacrifice to exploit a weak back rank – but Black's and not White's! This time, however, the consequences will be decisive.

21...♕xe5 22 ♘xf7+ 1-0

A Similar Game:

Navara – M. Ivanov
Icelandic Team Ch 2010/11
Philidor Defence

1 e4 d6 2 d4 ♘f6 3 ♘c3 e5 4 ♘f3 ♘bd7

A topical position in the Philidor Defence has been reached via a Pirc Defence, as this enables Black to avoid some move-order problems after 1 e4 e5 2 ♘f3 d6 3 d4 (see Game 15 for brief details). The central tension will be maintained by both sides as long as possible.

5 ♗c4 ♗e7 6 0-0 0-0 7 a4 c6 8 ♖e1 a5

By playing a4, White has stopped Black's natural plan of ...b5. This encourages Mikhail Ivanov to secure the c5-square for his knight before releasing the tension with ...exd4.

9 h3 exd4 10 ♕xd4!?

10 ♘xd4 is seen more often. Apparently though, White wants to put direct pressure on the d6-pawn.

10...♘c5 11 ♗f4

A natural follow-up of the plan. Black has to be careful not to lose his d-pawn. First of all, he aims to remove one of White's bishops.

11...♘e6 12 ♗xe6 ♗xe6 13 ♖ad1 ♘e8?! *(D)*

13...d5!? is a more ambitious approach.

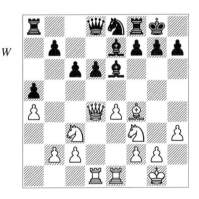

White has placed practically all of his pieces on their ideal squares. Now it's time to improve the knights' positions. But how?

14 ♕e3!

Just like Capablanca, White provides the d4-square for his knights. Before the text-move, Black's plan might have been to harass the queen with ...♗f6. With the retreat of the queen, however, this idea is prevented, since 14...♗f6 would be strongly met by 15 e5!.

14...♕b8 15 ♘d4 ♕a7 16 ♕g3 ♕c5

Black has found an interesting manoeuvre to land his queen on c5. Still, this does not prevent Navara from improving the position of his other knight.

17 ♘d5! *(D)*

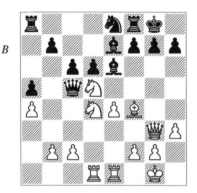

As normal, tactics are used to achieve strategic goals. For the moment, it is not possible to remove the apparently hanging knight: White has the upper hand after 17...cxd5 18 exd5 ♗xd5 (18...♕xd5? 19 ♘xe6) 19 ♖xe7, while after 17...♗xd5 18 exd5 the d5-pawn cannot be snatched, as the bishop on e7 is under attack.

In the light of these variations, Ivanov feels he must tolerate the knight on d5. But this decision allows one of the knights to establish itself

on the excellent f5-square, endangering Black's kingside.

17...♗d8 18 ♘e3 ♗f6 19 c3 ♖d8

Actually, it was possible to remove the knight at once with 19...♗xd4, but this would leave the d6-pawn even more vulnerable.

20 ♘df5 ♗xf5 21 ♘xf5 *(D)*

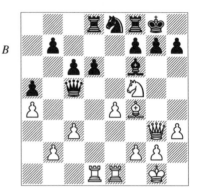

Thus, one of the knights has managed to land on the celebrated f5-square. All of White's pieces have reached their maximum potential, so it is time to reap the harvest!

21...♕c4 22 e5

This advance unlocks the door. After further exchanges, the g7-square will be sorely weak.

22...dxe5 23 ♖xd8 ♗xd8 24 ♗xe5 f6 25 ♗d6 1-0

A Game of Cat and Mouse

Game 15

E. Adams – C. Torre

New Orleans 1920

Philidor Defence

1 e4 e5 2 ♘f3 d6 3 d4 exd4

We have already seen in Game 7 (Tarrasch-Marco) the sort of problems that Black can face if he tries to maintain the tension in this type of structure. Still, it is not obligatory to exchange at such an early stage, and 3...♘d7 and 3...♘f6 are playable alternatives, even if there are some problems for Black in each case:

a) After 3...♘d7 4 ♗c4, Black must avoid pitfalls such as 4...♘gf6? 5 dxe5 ♘xe5 6 ♘xe5

dxe5 7 ♗xf7+! and 4...♗e7? 5 dxe5 ♘xe5 6 ♘xe5 dxe5 7 ♕h5, winning a pawn in both cases.

b) 3...♘f6 4 dxe5 initiates a forcing sequence that offers White an edge: 4...♘xe4 5 ♕d5 ♘c5 6 ♗g5 ♕d7 7 exd6.

4 ♕xd4

Her majesty can immediately join the battle, since White will pin the knight that would harass her.

4...♘c6 5 ♗b5 ♗d7 *(D)*

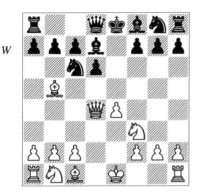

6 ♗xc6

In order to secure his queen's position in the centre, White is content to give up his bishop.

6...♗xc6 7 ♘c3 ♘f6 8 0-0

A more ambitious plan could be seen in 8 ♗g5 ♗e7 9 0-0-0.

8...♗e7 9 ♘d5

White plans further simplification, and we might expect this to lead to a dull position. Of course, he would have no objection to a dull but advantageous position...

9...♗xd5 10 exd5 0-0 11 ♗g5 c6

On the other hand, Black wants to increase the tension, as his opponent's space advantage is mostly provided by the d5-pawn, in addition to the well-placed queen on d4.

12 c4 cxd5

An '*elastic band*' trick might accelerate the simplification process: 12...♘xd5!? 13 cxd5 ♗xg5 14 ♘xg5 ♕xg5 15 dxc6 bxc6 16 ♕xd6 ♕b5. Although Black's pawn-structure is damaged, it is not possible to talk about a significant advantage in this major-piece endgame.

13 cxd5 ♖e8 14 ♖fe1 a5?!

The first step along the wrong path: Black desires to play ...♖c8, so he prepares this idea by securing his a-pawn first. Of course, rooks belong on open files. Still, it would be better to take White's upcoming pressure on the e-file into account: 14...h6 15 ♗h4 ♕d7 16 ♖e2 ♗d8 and potential problems on the open file can be resolved with simplifications.

15 ♖e2 ♖c8? 16 ♖ae1

Suddenly ♗xf6 followed by ♖xe8+ seems highly menacing.

16...♕d7 *(D)*

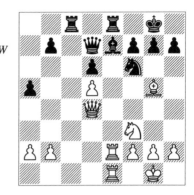

Black looks for salvation by connecting the rooks. Torre might be anticipating that 17 ♗xf6 ♗xf6, followed by rook exchanges, would lead to an equal game. Unfortunately, things are not that simple.

17 ♗xf6 ♗xf6 *(D)*

Actually, there is one more important factor in this position: both kings lack *luft* (i.e. escape-squares from the back rank, such as might be provided by playing h3/...h6). In this respect, his knight's control over e1 is an important trump for Adams, even though this isn't a cast-iron guarantee against back-rank problems.

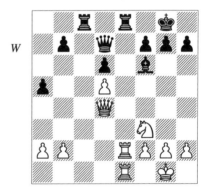

18 ♕g4!

Deflection it is! White exploits the fact that the e8-rook is somewhat loose. Therefore, he can repeatedly attack Black's queen, which is tied to protecting the rook. Suddenly the game will turn into a real game of cat and mouse.

18...♕b5

18...♕xg4 19 ♖xe8+ ♖xe8 20 ♖xe8#. This variation shows that Black's queen must not only move to save its own skin, but must find a square where it still covers the e8-rook.

19 ♕c4!

This time White's queen is 'sacrificed' on a square where not one, but two(!) different black pieces can dispose of her. Nonetheless, those two pieces both have to defend the e8-rook, so...

19...♕d7

...is forced. How should White continue to chase Black's queen?

20 ♕c7! *(D)*

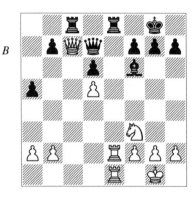

It seems that White's queen is not content to let her counterpart go yet!

20...♕b5 21 a4!

This move is important, as after the careless immediate capture 21 ♕xb7?, it is then Black who benefits from White's back-rank weakness: 21...♕xe2! 22 ♖xe2 ♖c1+ 23 ♖e1 ♖exe1+ 24 ♘xe1 ♖xe1#. The text-move, however, forces the black queen off the a6-f1 diagonal.

21...♕xa4 22 ♖e4 ♕b5

Thus we reach a similar position, with the exception being the rook's position on e4. This seemingly minor detail will leave Black's queen helpless.

23 ♕xb7 *(D)*

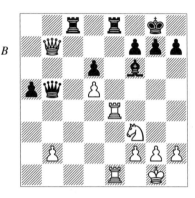

1-0

The back-rank weakness has never been a more decisive element.

The Immortal Zugzwang Game

Game 16
Sämisch – Nimzowitsch
Copenhagen 1923
Queen's Indian Defence

1 d4 ♘f6 2 c4 e6 3 ♘f3 b6

The *Queen's Indian Defence*. With this system, Black seeks to control the central light squares with his bishop from a distance.

4 g3 ♗b7 5 ♗g2 ♗e7 6 ♘c3 0-0 7 0-0

Both sides have developed their pieces in a logical manner, and Black now needs to find a constructive plan.

7...d5

With this move, Black firmly takes control of the important e4-square. On the negative

side, however, his light-squared bishop's diagonal is now blocked. This is one of the reasons why nowadays 7...♘e4 (and then, for example, 8 ♕c2 ♘xc3 9 ♕xc3) is seen more frequently.

8 ♘e5 c6 9 cxd5

Taking action in the centre with 9 e4 appears very plausible. After all, the b7-bishop's effect on the long diagonal has been reduced by Black's pawn moves.

9...cxd5!? *(D)*

This leads to a stable and rather pleasant structure for Black. Although capturing with 9...exd5 might appear more natural, it wouldn't be easy to develop the knight after White's reply 10 ♕a4. It also allows White the strong option of 10 e4 once again.

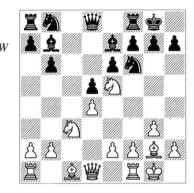

10 ♗f4 a6 11 ♖c1 b5 12 ♕b3 ♘c6

Black has completely focused on solving his queenside problems in his last few moves. The ...a6 and ...b5 advances have gained some space, as well as preparing to disturb the knight with a timely ...b4. The text-move seeks to exchange the undeveloped knight for its more active counterpart.

13 ♘xc6 ♗xc6 14 h3 ♕d7 15 ♔h2 (D)

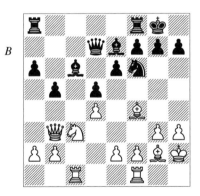

As the central structure is stable and the whole position is rather closed, White has a hard time finding a constructive plan. The same can also be said for Black, though Nimzowitsch succeeds in creating a productive strategy.

15...♘h5!

Now Black improves his position by gaining space on the kingside. This move wins a tempo by attacking the bishop (threatening to ruin White's pawn-structure), while unblocking the f-pawn.

16 ♗d2 f5

The first step towards the desired ...f4 advance.

17 ♕d1

Trying to stop his opponent's plan 'forever' with 17 e3 would result in a major headache for White: 17...b4! 18 ♘b1 ♗a4 (suddenly, White's queen faces serious problems finding a safe square) 19 ♕d3 ♗b5! and Black wins material with a *skewer* tactic. Instead, Sämisch retreats his queen to a square where it eyes the loose knight on h5. In this way he prepares the e4 advance.

17...b4

Using the whole board: Black pushes back the white knight while improving the light-squared bishop's view on the queenside.

18 ♘b1 ♗b5 19 ♖g1

White insists on discomforting the h5-knight by playing e4. But don't forget that Black has immensely improved his own position with his last few moves.

19...♗d6 20 e4 (D)

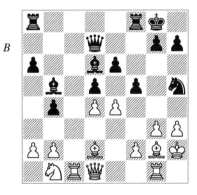

Either White or Black must be right in his claim. As is normally the case, it is the player whose pieces are better placed who can justify active play. And that is clearly Black, as a glance at the diagram position will prove. There are exceptional cases where the precise tactics favour the player who appears less well placed, but this is not one of those rare instances.

20...fxe4!

It turns out that Black can sacrifice his knight in return for massive positional compensation.

21 ♕xh5 ♖xf2 (D)

Black's active bishops are already exerting a lot of influence over the board, and now it is time for the black rooks to take the stage. Although White is material up, some of his pieces (especially the knight) are wholly out of play, and none are well-placed. That's why materialistic considerations are not that important in this specific battle.

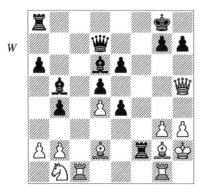

22 ♕g5 ♖af8 23 ♔h1 ♖8f5

Suddenly it becomes quite hard to find a safe place for the white queen.

24 ♕e3 ♗d3

Gradually narrowing the mobility range. It was possible to trap the queen with 24...♖e2 25 ♕b3 ♗a4, but Nimzowitsch's choice certainly doesn't spoil the advantage either.

25 ♖ce1

There isn't much difference between this move and 25 ♖ge1. The queen's insecurity is increasingly felt in either case.

25...h6

White is a piece up, but it is nearly impossible for him to find a single decent move: White is fast running out of moves that don't actually harm his own position. Indeed, Black could win most neatly by simply waiting for White to exhaust his supply of pawn moves, after which White would have to start ripping his own position apart. This type of situation is known as *zugzwang*, but it normally occurs in simplified endgames, rather than in the middlegame with a board full of pieces. It should also be noted that having seized control of g5, the ...♖5f3 idea has turned into a real threat, so Black has more than one way to win.

0-1

The game is often referred to as the *Immortal Zugzwang Game*.

Once the Tension has been Released

Game 17

Rubinstein – Hirschbein

Polish Ch, Lodz 1927

Queen's Gambit Declined

1 d4 ♘f6 2 c4 e6 3 ♘c3 d5

After this move, we have reached the characteristic position of the *Queen's Gambit Declined*. There are several move-orders to reach this opening, the most classical one being 1 d4 d5 2 c4 e6 3 ♘c3 ♘f6.

One of White's main objectives in this opening is to make it hard for Black to activate his light-squared bishop, which has been blocked in by his own central pawns standing on light squares.

4 ♗g5 ♗e7 5 e3 0-0 6 ♘f3 ♘bd7 (D)

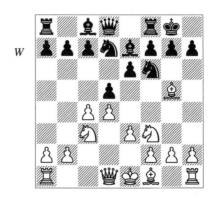

7 ♖c1

Both sides tailor their play around the possibility of Black playing ...dxc4. For example, White delays developing his light-squared bishop, since he would prefer to recapture on c4 by playing ♗xc4 in one move. Instead, a sequence such as 7 ♗d3 dxc4 8 ♗xc4 would be a loss of a tempo for White. Therefore he seeks useful moves that improve his position, such as 7 ♖c1, without making it easy for Black to resolve the central tension in a favourable manner.

7...c6 8 ♕c2

Continuing with *useful semi-waiting* moves. In his own 'waiting process', it is harder for Black to find constructive moves, since he lacks space.

8...♖e8 9 a3 *(D)*

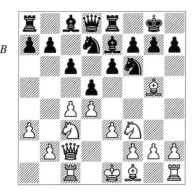

White manages to find another handy move: after ...dxc4, ♗xc4 the ...b5 advance will gain a tempo to develop the c8-bishop. The text-move prepares a good route (♗a2-b1) for the bishop in that case.

9...h6

The pawn-push at the other edge of the board with 9...a6 could also be considered: no matter what White plays, Black would then take the pawn with ...dxc4, followed by ...b5.

10 ♗f4 dxc4

Hirschbein didn't see much point in preserving the tension any longer. Usually, releasing the tension by initiating a sequence of exchanges results in improving one of the opponent's pieces. In our case, we can see that the f1-bishop can join the game without even losing a single tempo. In addition to this, Black has not yet found a way to activate his light-squared bishop.

11 ♗xc4 *(D)*

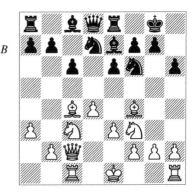

11...♘b6?

The mere fact that a move threatens an enemy piece is not sufficient in itself to render the move desirable. The move played also needs to be in accordance with the overall game plan, or to cause the opponent genuine inconvenience (and as we have noted, White has already prepared a good onward route for his c4-bishop).

Black should be trying to solve the standard problem of his passive light-squared bishop, which is behind the central pawn-chain. For instance, he could play 11...b6. The text-move, however, makes it even harder to develop the c8-bishop by blocking Black's b-pawn. In addition, on d7 the knight was well-placed to support the freeing pawn advances ...c5 and ...e5, which will now be very hard to achieve.

12 ♗a2

This is possible thanks to 9 a3.

12...♗d6

Piece-play in the centre by 12...♘bd5 would be a lesser evil. The exchange of dark-squared bishops is not necessarily favourable for Black. Exchanging pieces when in a cramped position is often a good idea, but less so if it costs time and merely highlights the difference in quality between the remaining pieces.

13 ♗xd6 ♕xd6 14 0-0

A '*simple chess*' approach has brought White an advantageous position. His space advantage, central pawn-majority and the c8-bishop's continuing problems are the main reasons for this evaluation.

14...♘bd7 *(D)*

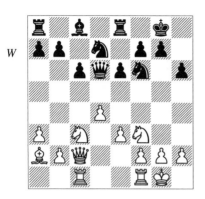

15 ♖fd1!

With his last move, Black admitted that the earlier 11...♘b6 was a dubious decision, but the resulting loss of time cannot be easily undone. White, on the other hand, improves his pieces one by one.

15...♕e7 *(D)*

After all his preparations, White was now ready to make the desired e4 advance. Hirschbein aims to meet this idea with ...e5, even though this opens the a2-bishop's diagonal. Therefore, the queen leaves the d-file, so it will not be facing the d1-rook after exchanges on e5.

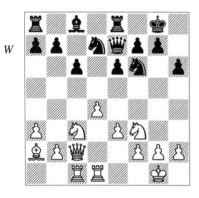

16 ♘e5

White is looking to seize the initiative. This move is highly 'committal', since it changes the pawn-structure, and hence the whole character of the position.

16...♘xe5

Hirschbein refuses to tolerate such a strong knight in the centre. He aims to find at least

some counterplay (which he has not seen since the beginning of the game!) by putting pressure on White's upcoming e5-pawn.

17 dxe5 ♘g4

The advanced e5-pawn cramps Black's position significantly. However, if White were to become tied down to this pawn, it could easily turn into a liability for White. Of course, it is not possible to protect the pawn with 18 f4?, as this leaves the e3-pawn *en prise*. However, Rubinstein is in no rush to defend the pawn. He instead creates a much more dangerous threat of his own.

18 ♗b1 g6 *(D)*

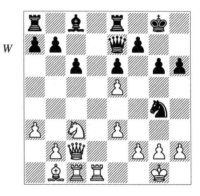

In a chess game, there is often a critical moment when we must make a decision upon which the fate of the entire game hinges. This is such a position. White could simply protect his pawn, but such a 'timid' approach not only misses the opportunity for an advantage, but also it could even yield a slight plus for Black: 19 ♕e4? ♕h4! 20 ♕f4 g5! 21 ♕g3 ♕xg3 22 hxg3 ♘xe5.

19 ♘e4!

An outstanding evaluation. Rubinstein vacates the c3-square for his queen, and at the same time forces his opponent to grab the pawn, as now ♘d6 and ♘f6+ are quite unpleasant threats.

19...♘xe5

Unwillingly removing the pawn. This capture will lead to serious problems on the dark squares, which have already been significantly weakened by the exchange of bishops and the ...g6 advance.

20 ♕c3! *(D)*

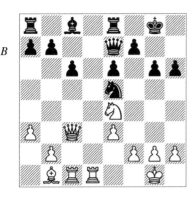

Now Black cannot maintain his knight on e5, where it serves the important function of blocking the long diagonal. After it moves, White will be able to conquer the f6-square with deadly effect.

20...♘d7

White wins after both 20...f6 21 f4 ♘g4 22 h3 f5 23 ♘d6 and 20...f5 21 ♘d6, showing that d6 as well as f6 is a target for the knight.

21 ♖xd7! 1-0

After the removal of the 'guardian', the ♘f6+ idea is decisive: 21...♗xd7 22 ♘f6+ ♔f8 23 ♘d5! threatens ♕h8# and the black queen.

Open Up the Lines!

Game 18
Glücksberg – Najdorf
Warsaw 1930
Dutch Defence

1 d4 f5 2 c4 ♘f6 3 ♘c3 e6 4 ♘f3 d5 5 e3 c6 *(D)*

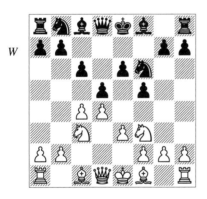

A form of the *Stonewall Dutch*. With this system, Black seeks a closed and solid centre by putting all his central pawns on light squares. Especially his control over the e4-square stands out. Still, like all defensive systems, it has its drawbacks: the e5-square is a 'hole', and the light-squared bishop is behind the pawn-chain and some effort will be needed to activate it.

6 ♗d3 ♗d6 7 0-0 0-0 8 ♘e2

Because Black's sole defender of the dark squares is his dark-squared bishop, White seeks to exchange off this piece. But as the queen's knight has already been developed to c3, it is hard to carry out the well-known plan of b3 and ♗a3.

8...♘bd7 9 ♘g5? *(D)*

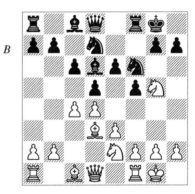

Trying to win a tempo by attacking the e6-pawn, and thereby gaining time to play f4. But one should never forget that it is very important to give attention to our opponent's ideas, as well as our own plans.

9...♗xh2+!

A simple tactic that wins a pawn: 10 ♔xh2 ♘g4+, followed by ...♕xg5.

10 ♔h1 ♞g4!

Black correctly brings more pieces to the kingside, rather than taking care of his threatened e6-pawn.

11 f4

It wouldn't be possible for White to endure the assault after 11 ♞xe6 ♛h4.

11...♛e8

As the queen's desired route d8-h4 has been blocked, Najdorf changes its path to the h-file.

12 g3

In his turn, Glücksberg seeks salvation by leaving the h-file immediately.

12...♛h5 13 ♔g2

Both sides have implemented their respective plans. White's hopes rely on posing some problems on the h-file with moves like ♖h1 and ♞f3. Of course, this could only be possible if Black fails to find a constructive plan. However, Najdorf comes up with an excellent strategy, and he follows this method right to the end of the game: *open up the lines*!

13...♝g1!

An instructive way to open the h-file. Now both 14 ♖xg1 and 14 ♔xg1 allow mate, but what happens if he takes with the knight?

14 ♞xg1 ♛h2+ 15 ♔f3 *(D)*

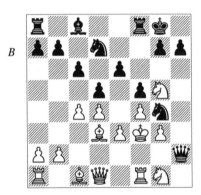

Thus, the king had no choice but to move towards the centre after the bishop sacrifice. Still, in order to benefit from this occurrence, the paths to White's king have to be opened up!

15...e5!!

After this marvellous move, nearly all Black's pieces join the assault. More importantly, the pawn-shield that provides safety to White's king for the moment will be torn apart.

16 dxe5

As 16...e4+ 17 ♝xe4 fxe4+ 18 ♞xe4 ♞de5+! 19 dxe5 ♞xe5# was a serious concrete threat, the sacrifice has to be accepted.

16...♞dxe5+ 17 fxe5 ♞xe5+ 18 ♔f4 ♞g6+ 19 ♔f3

After a more or less forced sequence of moves, we reach another critical position. Although the king's defences have been ripped apart by successive sacrifices, Black has to continue playing accurately; let's not forget that he is material down. However, the strategy that leads to glory is always the same: in order to benefit from the king's exposed position, lines must be opened!

19...f4!

The importance of the e5-square is emphasized once again, with the threat of ...♞e5#.

20 exf4 *(D)*

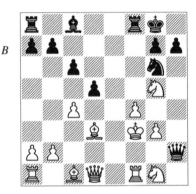

White at least tries to vacate e3 as an escape-route for his king. However, this is a futile effort, since it will be impossible to defend the position once Black's remaining pieces join the attack.

20...♝g4+!

After the star move 15...e5!!, it has been clear that nearly all Black's forces will join the assault. This bishop sacrifice has to be accepted because of the *skewer*, but this will lead to White's king moving even further up the board.

21 ♔xg4 ♞e5+!

What a surprise(!): Black opens lines. The knight is sacrificed to clear the f-file.

22 fxe5 h5# (0-1)

The final position is the proof of the rightfulness of Black's consistent strategy in this game.

Those Isolated Queen's Pawns...

Game 19

Botvinnik – Vidmar

Nottingham 1936

Queen's Gambit Declined

1 c4

Although the game has started with the move 1 c4, which symbolizes the English Opening, it will swiftly transpose to Queen's Gambit waters.

1...e6 2 ♘f3 d5 3 d4 ♘f6 *(D)*

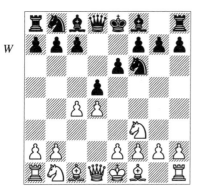

4 ♗g5 ♗e7 5 ♘c3

A conventional move-order to reach this position is 1 d4 d5 2 c4 e6 3 ♘c3 ♘f6 4 ♗g5 ♗e7 5 ♘f3.

5...0-0 6 e3 ♘bd7

Black determines the course of the game by giving priority to developing his knight. Another major option here is the Tartakower Defence with 6...h6 7 ♗h4 b6, which mainly focuses on trying to solve the light-squared bishop's problem by developing it on the long diagonal.

7 ♗d3 c5

This advance suddenly increases the tension between the pawns, and therefore comes along with some risks. Apparently Botvinnik thinks it best to preserve the central status quo for the moment, and castles kingside, to be better ready for whatever developments may now occur.

8 0-0 cxd4 9 exd4 dxc4 10 ♗xc4 *(D)*

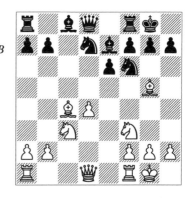

After all the exchanges, a typical 'isolated queen's pawn' position has been reached. Isolated pawns – ones that lack any friendly pawns on the adjacent files – can easily turn into weaknesses in the long run. This is because they can't be protected by other pawns, and so rely on piece support, and in general pieces should perform more major tasks than merely defend pawns. But an isolated queen's pawn in a structure like the one we have here provides a space advantage and attacking opportunities to its owner, as well as controlling some key squares such as e5. So, it is a double-edged element that directly creates imbalance on the board.

10...♘b6

This natural move, in addition to threatening the bishop, aims to establish firm control over the d5-square.

11 ♗b3 ♗d7

Now Black plans to strengthen his control over d5 with ...♗c6. Both sides have played rather logically so far.

12 ♕d3

On the other hand, White creates a classical attacking weapon by lining up his queen and bishop on the b1-h7 diagonal. Also, as we shall soon see in the game, the queen is ready for a possible switch to the kingside via the third rank. Still, there were other possible approaches here. For example, Black's control over e5 has been weakened by ...♘b6, and White could try to benefit from this by centralizing a knight with 12 ♘e5.

12...♘bd5 13 ♘e5 ♗c6

We see that some of the aforementioned ideas are put to use, although in a different order.

14 ♖ad1 ♘b4?! *(D)*

In isolated queen's pawn structures, exchanging off the opponent's most effective pieces is an important defensive plan. 14...♖c8 might be a good preparation for such an idea: then 15 ♗c2 is not very appropriate, as there is 15...♘b4 in reply. 15 ♕h3 (White's next move in the game continuation) needs careful handling because 15...♘xc3?! 16 bxc3 is tricky for Black since 16...♗d5 17 c4! and 16...♗e4 17 ♖fe1 ♗f5 18 ♕f3 are both awkward. 15...h6 looks risky, but 16 ♗xh6 is far from clear, while if the bishop retreats, then Black can consider offering to exchange some minor pieces.

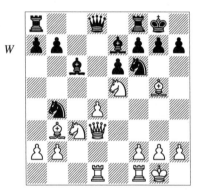

Although Black has placed his knight on b4 with a concrete goal, this piece will soon have to return to d5, after several strong moves by White.

15 ♕h3!

Eyeing the e6- and h7-squares.

15...♗d5

Why is this blockading idea ineffective here? Because the c3-knight is available to eliminate the 'balancer' of the position, Black's light-squared bishop.

16 ♘xd5! ♘bxd5 17 f4! *(D)*

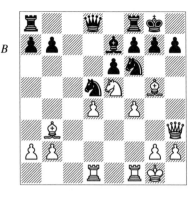

While keeping all his powerful attacking pieces on the board, White strengthens his assault with his reserves. The vulnerability of the e6-square has been emphasized with the ♕d3-h3 manoeuvre. Now Botvinnik aims to put further pressure on this point with the f5 advance.

17...♖c8

Bringing the rook into action, while at the same time stopping ♗c2. However, Black's seemingly solid position has already lost its dynamism; he is now merely parrying White's active plans. On the other hand, White's pieces constantly improve their positions and thereby increase the pressure on Black.

18 f5 exf5 19 ♖xf5 *(D)*

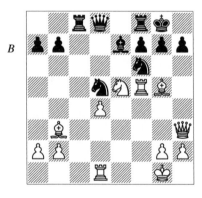

After this last exchange, the power of the unopposed b3-bishop is increasingly felt in Black's camp. Now ♗h6!! is an incredible threat.

19...♕d6?!

It is easy to criticize nearly all of Black's moves in this tough position. But it would be fairer to look for the mistakes in his previous moves. Alekhine, the 4th World Chess Champion, mentions that 19...♖c7 deserves attention. Yet in his notes, he also points out that the pressure would continue with 20 ♖df1. 20 ♗h6, with ♖g5 ideas, is also powerful.

Now Botvinnik strikes on the a2-g8 diagonal.

20 ♘xf7!

First Black's light-squared bishop, then the e6-pawn, and finally the f7-pawn have been eliminated. All these actions have taken place to benefit maximally from White's own light-squared bishop.

20...♖xf7 21 ♗xf6

Now the guardian of the d5-knight is removed.

21...♗xf6 22 ♖xd5

White is a pawn up, but his advantage is of a far greater and more violent nature than that. With his consistent play, Botvinnik has made the b3-bishop's influence the decisive factor in this game. Now it's time to seal the deal.

22...♕c6 *(D)*

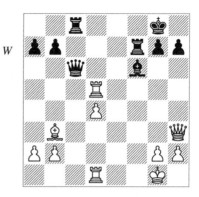

23 ♖d6 ♕e8 24 ♖d7

Once again reminding us who is the 'boss' of this game.

1-0

Safety First!

Game 20
Smyslov – Kottnauer
Groningen 1946
Sicilian Defence

1 e4 c5 2 ♘f3 d6 3 d4 cxd4 4 ♘xd4 ♘f6 5 ♘c3 a6 6 ♗e2 e6 *(D)*

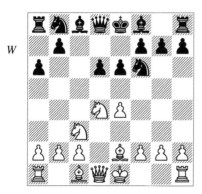

The game has started with a *Najdorf* move-order (5...a6), but Black has chosen a *Scheveningen* pawn-structure with ...d6 and ...e6. In this sharp opening system, Black embraces a kind of a 'zone defence' strategy, controlling all the squares from b5 to f5.

7 0-0 b5?!

Of course ...b5 is an essential part of Black's game-plan, which mainly aims to exert pressure in the centre, while gaining some space on the queenside. But wouldn't it be a mistake to forget that such an advance, without first completing development or bringing the king into safety, comes along with major risks?

8 ♗f3!

Although winning some space in the centre with f4 is the most natural follow-up in the Scheveningen, Smyslov wants to threaten his opponent directly with 9 e5. Quite a concrete plan, isn't it? Suddenly, the focal point of the struggle will turn to the queenside, which has been somewhat weakened by Black's untimely 7...b5?!.

8...♖a7 (D)

8...♘fd7 would be met by 9 e5 d5 10 ♘xd5! exd5 11 ♗xd5, when White is much better. The attempt to close the diagonal by 8...e5 weakens d5 and White would take an unquestionable command of this square with 9 ♘f5 g6 10 ♘e3 ♗e6 11 a4! b4 12 ♘cd5.

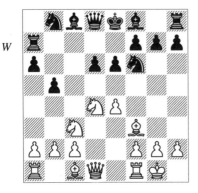

9 ♕e2 ♖c7 10 ♖d1

The e5 idea is prepared once again, with the emergence of the pin along the d-file.

10...♘bd7 11 a4! (D)

When choosing a plan, we should consider where our pieces' energy is most keenly felt. In this sense, beginning with 8 ♗f3!, Smyslov has directed his attention to the queenside, which his opponent exposed with an untimely advance. Now White aims to weaken the pawn-chain.

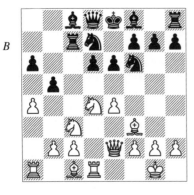

11...bxa4

11...b4 12 ♘a2 would leave the pawn vulnerable, because against 12...a5, there comes the reply 13 ♘b5.

12 ♘xa4 ♗b7

Normally 12...♗e7 followed by ...0-0 right away would be a good plan. But against this, 13 ♗d2 intending ♗a5 would be strong.

13 e5!

Opening lines against Black's uncastled king. There are now many possible sequences of captures, which require precise analysis.

13...♘xe5 (D)

Black has other options, but none of them seem bright: 13...♗xf3 14 ♘xf3 dxe5 15 ♘xe5 ♕c8 16 ♗f4! and White is unquestionably better as 16...♖xc2? fails to 17 ♖ac1!; 13...dxe5 14 ♗xb7 ♖xb7 15 ♕xa6 ♕c8 16 ♘c6 and once again, White has the upper hand as 16...♖c7 is strongly met by 17 ♘b6!.

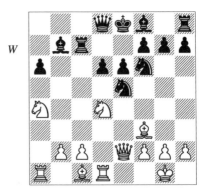

14 ♗xb7 ♖xb7 15 ♕xa6

Maintaining the pressure on Black's queenside. Black has already lost his a- and b-pawns, and will now come under attack from White's queen and knights.

15...♕b8 16 ♘c6! (D)

Constant pressure! It is essential to continue with forcing moves, to deny the opponent any chance to organize his defences.

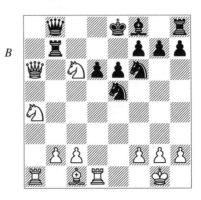

16...♘xc6 17 ♕xc6+ ♘d7

17...♖d7 loses to 18 ♘b6, when White wins material.

18 ♘c5!! *(D)*

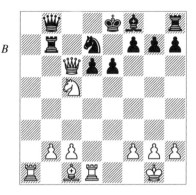

A great blow, which benefits from the pin and opens the d-file and h2-b8 diagonal. Of course it is obligatory for Black to accept the offer.

18...dxc5 19 ♗f4

Development with tempo leaves Black helpless.

19...♗d6

19...♕xf4 20 ♕xb7 and White wins.

20 ♗xd6 ♖b6 *(D)*

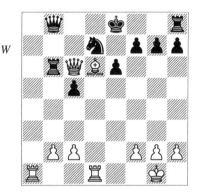

A last desperate try.

21 ♕xd7+! 1-0

Kottnauer resigned because 21...♔xd7 22 ♗xb8+ leaves Black a piece down.

The Double Bishop Sacrifice
Game 21
Kirilov – Furman
Vilnius 1949
Ruy Lopez

1 e4 e5 2 ♘f3 ♘c6 3 ♗b5 a6 4 ♗a4 ♘f6 5 ♕e2

See Roesch-Schlage, Hamburg 1910 (Game 11).

5...b5 6 ♗b3 ♗e7 7 a4 *(D)*

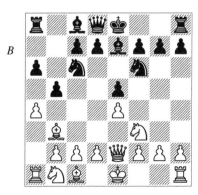

In the Ruy Lopez, it is quite common to attack Black's queenside pawn-chain with this advance. White aims to force his opponent to make a concession – either a weakness in the pawn-structure, or a weak square.

7...b4 8 ♗d5?!

This move tries to benefit from the vulnerability of the e5-pawn, yet it is unnecessarily ambitious. So far, Black has not made any single mistake that can be punished. Therefore, it was better to continue with normal development.

A series of exchanges now simplifies the position.

8...♘xd5

It was hard to tolerate the pin.

9 exd5 ♘d4 10 ♘xd4 exd4 11 0-0

An important question is whether White could hunt down the d4-pawn with 11 ♕e4. There follows 11...♗b7 12 ♕xd4 0-0 13 0-0 a5, when Black obtains reasonable chances with his bishop-pair, as White has some problems due to his lack of queenside development. This line was probably the reason behind Kirilov's choice, by which he seeks to secure his king.

11...0-0 12 ♕c4?! *(D)*

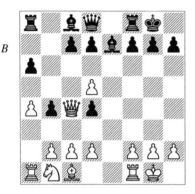

After a slight delay, White harasses the d4-pawn. As the loss of this pawn is inevitable, Furman opens up the position, so that his bishop-pair can be maximally effective.

12...c5!

In order to open more lines, the d7-pawn is offered instead of the one on d4.

13 dxc6

Risky, yet after 13 d3 a5, Black would not face any difficulties whatsoever.

13...dxc6 14 ♕xc6 ♖a7 *(D)*

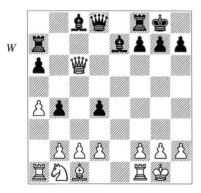

The forced sequence of moves has ended, and now it is a good time to make an evaluation of this concrete position. At first glance, it might

seem that White has been rewarded for his ambitious choice to exert pressure against Black's pawns with 8 ♗d5?! – he has an extra pawn, after all. But there is a cost. The position is very open, and Black has obtained the bishop-pair. The most important element in this position is White's lack of queenside development. Therefore, it is likely that Black has more than enough compensation for his small material deficit.

15 ♕f3 ♖c7 16 d3 ♗b7!

Regaining the pawn with 16...♖xc2 was also possible, but development is far more important.

17 ♕d1 ♗d6

Black's bishops are lining up menacingly against White's king. Kirilov brings some of his reserves into the defence without losing any time.

18 ♘d2 ♖e8?!

Immediately going for an all-out attack with 18...♕h4 could be more effective.

19 ♘c4? *(D)*

It was time to give up the material advantage, and to try to eliminate at least one of the bishops with 19 ♘e4!.

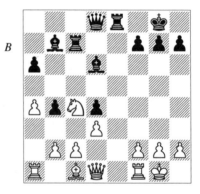

But apparently for a moment, Kirilov has forgotten that he has developed his knight for defensive purposes. Consequently, he loses to a standard series of sacrifices that has been well-known since Em.Lasker-J.Bauer, Amsterdam 1889 (see Supplementary Game 1).

19...♗xh2+!

The king has been left to fend for itself against the assault of Black's pieces. Its pawn-shield will be torn apart with two bishop sacrifices. The first sacrifice removes one pawn and gains time to bring the queen into the attack.

We should note that 19...罩xc4! 20 dxc4 豐h4 is also very strong (e.g., 21 f4 ♗c5 or 21 h3 罩e6!).

20 ♔xh2 豐h4+ 21 ♔g1 ♗xg2! *(D)*

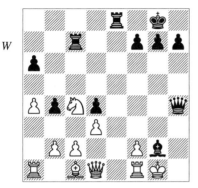

This second bishop sacrifice opens the g-file for the use of a black rook.

22 ♔xg2 罩c6!

The goal of this final step is rather obvious: after the *rook-lift*, White's king will be helpless.

23 ♗f4

White gives up his bishop so that he can escape via the f1-square. But in a couple of moves, another weakness will emerge.

23...豐xf4 24 罩h1 罩f6!

How can White defend f2?

25 罩h2 罩g6+! 0-1

Now 26 ♔h1 fails due to a tactical theme, *deflection*: 26...罩e1+! 27 豐xe1 豐f3+ (according to some sources, White resigned here) 28 罩g2 豐xg2#.

As Long as the King is Stuck in the Centre...

Game 22
Spassky – Avtonomov
Leningrad Junior Ch 1949
Queen's Gambit Accepted

1 d4 d5 2 c4 dxc4

The *Queen's Gambit Accepted*. Black allows his opponent to acquire quite a strong formation in the centre. But in return, he aims to solve his light-squared bishop's development problem. While White is spending time recapturing the c4-pawn, a standard plan for Black is to expand on the queenside with ...a6, ...b5 and ...♗b7.

3 ♘f3

Directly attacking c4 with 3 e4 is another story. Apparently Spassky does not want to give his opponent a possible 'freeing' opportunity with 3...e5.

3...♘f6 4 e3 e6 5 ♗xc4 c5

So far, both sides have followed opening theory. After White has recaptured his pawn, Black tries to put d4 under pressure, in order to prevent the desired e4 advance.

6 0-0 a6 7 豐e2 *(D)*

Since the beginning of the game, one of Black's main objectives was ...b5. White could

easily stop this plan with 7 a4. But Spassky's set-up with 豐e2 and 罩d1 is both very logical and typical: now the e4 advance would be more effective, since it will put Black's queen in an uncomfortable position.

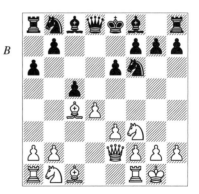

7...b5 8 ♗b3 ♘c6

Who would have thought that Avtonomov's decision on this move would shape the course of the whole game? Although 8...c4 would have won a tempo, this advance releases the pressure on d4, and this makes it easier for White to play e4 at the right moment. But 8...♗b7 is more flexible: in this way, Black can decide later on how best to develop the b8-knight, once White has committed to a particular set-up.

9 ♘c3 cxd4 *(D)*

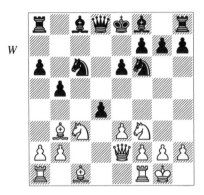

10 ♖d1!?

Rooks belong on open files. In the Queen's Gambit Accepted, the ♖fd1 idea can be seen quite frequently. 10 exd4!? is also possible, when we can see this rook move once again: 10...♘xd4?! 11 ♘xd4 ♕xd4 12 ♘d5!? ♘xd5 (12...♗d6 is a better option) 13 ♖d1. In principle, the main objective is to harass Black's queen on the open file.

10...♗b7

It is unrealistic for Black to try to keep his material advantage when he has neither castled nor completed his development. Avtonomov is well aware of the fact that his pawn advantage is temporary. Still, it seems that giving priority to kingside development was better, since this approach could also help him castle. Therefore, 10...♗e7, followed by ...0-0, seems like a much safer option.

11 exd4

An *isolated queen's pawn* structure has arisen. A sharp and unbalanced struggle awaits both sides. An IQP gives its possessor some advantages by controlling space and providing active posts in the opening and middlegame, but it can easily turn into a liability in the endgame.

11...♘b4 *(D)*

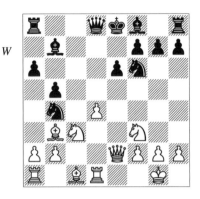

A basic (yet usually effective!) strategy when facing an isolated queen's pawn is to blockade this pawn with a minor piece. The reason is rather simple: the blockading piece cannot be attacked by a pawn. It is quite obvious that Black has prepared ...♘bd5 with his last move. But as we've mentioned so many times throughout the book, the opponent's ideas are at least as important as our own.

12 d5!!

In order to benefit from the black king's insecure posture in the centre, it is very important to open lines. Therefore Spassky does not hesitate to sacrifice his d-pawn; if he had waited even a single move, Black could have blockaded the pawn and the fleeting chance for its advance would have disappeared.

12...♘bxd5 13 ♗g5 ♗e7 14 ♗xf6! *(D)*

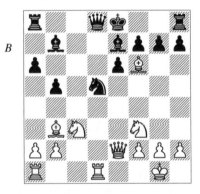

Another point of ♕e2 can be seen: it's not possible to recapture with the bishop, since 14...♗xf6 15 ♘xd5 costs Black a piece due to the pin on the e-file. Therefore Black must accept a fractured pawn-structure on the kingside.

14...gxf6 15 ♘xd5 ♗xd5 16 ♗xd5 exd5 17 ♘d4 *(D)*

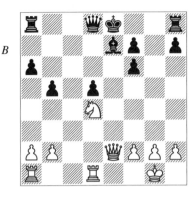

B

White has only sacrificed a mere pawn to reach this wonderful position. Black's pawn-structure is a wreck, and it is entirely possible for White to step up pressure on the e-file with ♘f5. Avtonomov, totally in desperation, tries to evade the pin.

17...♔f8 18 ♘f5 h5

Facing mortal threats, Black stops ♕h5-h6+.

19 ♖xd5!

Overloading Black's queen, which is defending the bishop on e7.

19...♕xd5 20 ♕xe7+ ♔g8 21 ♕xf6

As Black is helpless against ♕g7#...

1-0

A Similar Case:

Gipslis – Darznieks
Latvian Ch, Riga 1962
Position after 11...♘d7-f6?

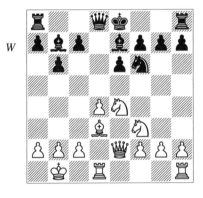

W

Black aims to achieve a rather balanced position with the help of simplifications. However, his last move was a mistake. The idea itself was perfectly reasonable, but it should have been prepared with 11...0-0, which is always an important safety measure. After witnessing Spassky's approach in a similar position, White's play won't be that surprising any more.

12 ♘xf6+!

A key guardian of the important d5-square is removed.

12...gxf6

Black hopes to prevent the d5 advance by keeping the e-file closed.

13 d5! exd5

More or less forced, since 13...♗xd5 fails to 14 ♗b5+ c6 15 ♗xc6+!.

14 ♘d4 c5 *(D)*

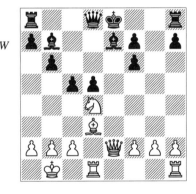

W

15 ♘f5

You should be familiar with all these manoeuvres!

15...♗c8 16 ♗b5+ ♔f8 17 ♖xd5! ♕c7 18 ♖d7! 1-0

The rook's interference tactic brings the game to an end.

Weak Squares

Game 23
Boleslavsky – Smyslov
Budapest Candidates 1950
Slav Defence

1 d4 d5 2 c4 c6

The *Slav Defence*. Black supports the d5-pawn without closing his light-squared bishop's diagonal. In addition to this, after a possible ...dxc4, he aims to make it more difficult for White to recapture his pawn, by threatening the ...b5 advance.

3 ②c3 ②f6 4 ②f3

Boleslavsky gives priority to developing his knights.

4...dxc4 *(D)*

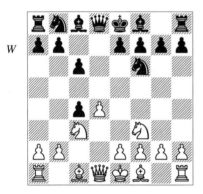

5 a4

This most popular move's goal is obvious: stopping ...b5. This makes sure White can recapture the c4-pawn, but the a-pawn's advance isn't such a useful move in itself, and can even prove weakening in some lines. On the other hand, Black's ...c6 isn't the most useful move either, so this is a typical trade-off.

5...c5!?

This interesting approach is rarely seen. Apparently with his bold move, Smyslov is aiming to prevent his opponent from acquiring a strong pawn-majority in the centre. The standard move is 5...②f5 and only after developing the bishop, ...e6.

6 e4

A natural way to grab space, though 6 d5 is also a logical reply.

6...cxd4 7 ♕xd4

When playing with the white pieces, many players are unwilling to exchange queens at such an early stage. But I don't have any idea how White might win the c4-pawn back after 7 ②xd4 e5 8 ②db5 a6! (even better than taking castling rights from White with 8...♕xd1+) 9 ♕xd8+ ♔xd8 10 ②a3 ♗xa3! 11 ♖xa3 ♗e6.

7...♕xd4 8 ②xd4 *(D)*

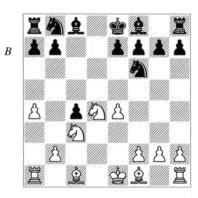

In this 'queenless middlegame' White has some trumps: after ②db5, some fork ideas will appear. Also, it is hard to find a suitable square for Black's light-squared bishop. Still, White should be careful not to create a very dry and dull position by further simplification. If he is to make anything of his slight pluses, he must identify some forcing dynamic resources.

8...e6 9 ②db5 ②a6 10 ♗xc4

White has managed to take his pawn back with a slightly superior position.

10...♗c5 11 ♗f4 ♔e7

It is always easy to criticize one side's play after seeing the whole battle. But during the game, each critical decision is made under different circumstances. In many queenless middlegame positions, both sides keep their kings in the centre, rather than adopting a 'safety-first' approach by castling. If the queenless middlegame is transformed into a true endgame (by further exchanges and/or a lessening of the importance of dynamic factors), then the kings need to be ready to play an active role. Still, Black has not completely coordinated his pieces and it is legitimate to question the 7th World Champion's decision.

12 0-0 ♗d7 *(D)*

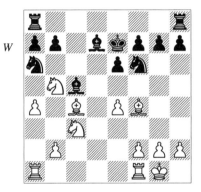

13 e5!

An important moment: the f6-knight is exiled to an ineffective square, whereas the e4-square has been prepared for the use of White's own knight. Also, the d6-square has turned into an outpost for the future.

13...♘h5

Knights stuck on the edge of the board are often ineffective and this matter has been emphasized since Tarrasch's era: "a knight on the rim is dim". A knight's mobility is severely restricted when it is located on the edge. In this case, the knight attacks White's bishop, but this is only a temporary issue and in a couple of moves, the knight will turn into a burden.

14 ♗e3!

A voluntary invitation to 'wreck' the pawn-structure requires a deep positional understanding. For the upcoming unbalanced position, Boleslavsky has appreciated that his play along the half-open f-file (a dynamic element) is much more important than the structural damage (a static element).

For the moment, the exchange of bishops is not obligatory. But the tension on the board is

constantly increasing, and with his more harmonious pieces, White is better prepared for this development.

14...♖hc8 *(D)*

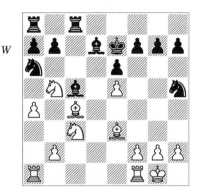

15 ♗e2

Defence and attack: bishop runs away from the black rook's attack, and at the same time harasses the h5-knight.

15...g6 16 ♘e4 *(D)*

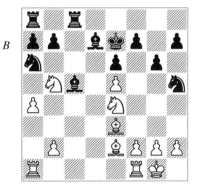

16...♗xe3

Smyslov sees that his dark squares have been weakened by the forced 15...g6. In order to reduce his problems on these squares, he removes White's dark-squared bishop. But White now will gain his longed-for play on the f-file.

17 fxe3 ♖c2

Seeking counterplay with active moves is the way to go, but even this will not be sufficient.

18 ♘bd6!

The pressure on f7 makes the bishop taboo: 18...♖xe2? 19 ♖xf7+ ♔d8 20 ♖f8+ (even 20 ♘xb7+ is good) 20...♔c7 21 ♖xa8 gives White both a positional and a material advantage. Therefore, the f7-square must be defended.

18...♖f8 *(D)*

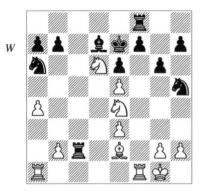

19 ♗xa6

Why eliminate the knight when it is so ineffective? In order to sustain the initiative, my dear...

19...bxa6 20 g4 ♘g7

A miserable square for the knight.

21 ♘f6

A picture of total domination. Threats of ♘xh7, followed by ♖xf7+, are in the air.

21...♗c6 22 ♖fc1! 1-0

The removal of the only active piece puts an end to Black's futile hopes of salvation. This instructive game is the first example in Sergiu Samarian's highly-praised work, *Das Systematische Schachtraining*.

Lack of Development

Game 24
Soultanbéieff – Dubyna
Liège 1953
Queen's Indian Defence

1 d4 ♘f6 2 c4 e6 3 ♘f3 b6 4 e3

In the Queen's Indian Defence, the interaction between the opposing pieces is sometimes delayed until the early middlegame phase. As a result, White has a free hand for choosing the most suitable option to his taste. Although his choice leaves his own dark-squared bishop behind the pawn-chain, Soultanbéieff apparently wants to create a strong pawn-centre.

4...♗b7 5 ♗d3 ♗e4?!

This move is very hard to understand and explain: spending time voluntarily exchanging the bishop that is an integral part of Black's whole set-up cannot be good. Probably Dubyna was aiming to prevent the e4 advance (a reasonable motivation, but this is not yet a threat, and there will be better ways to prevent it, such as ...d5), or he wanted to eliminate White's own light-squared bishop.

6 ♘c3 ♗b4

Increasing Black's control over the light squares by pinning the knight is very natural. But because of the dubious decision on the

previous move, it will be quite hard for Black's minor pieces to maintain their control over these critical squares.

7 ♕c2 *(D)*

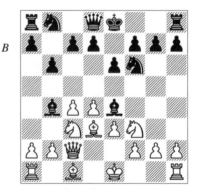

Consequently, White immediately hits e4 and forces matters.

7...♗xd3 8 ♕xd3 d5

Otherwise White would gain total control over the centre after the e4 advance.

9 cxd5! *(D)*

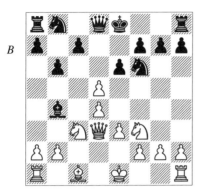

After this timely capture, Black fails to maintain his presence in the centre, because his bishop would easily drop off (9...exd5?? 10 ♕b5+, followed by 11 ♕xb4, winning). Even the *zwischenzug* (in-between move) 9...♗xc3+ is insufficient, as White's ♗a3 idea after 10 bxc3 exd5 would hinder Black from castling, and also White could once again launch an attack on Black's central foothold with the c4 advance.

9...♘xd5 10 0-0

This brings the king to safety, as well as leaving the b4-bishop and d5-knight aimless.

10...♘xc3

Although Black loses a tempo with this capture, in the alternative variation 10...♗xc3 11 bxc3, the ♗a3 idea would emerge once again to trouble Black.

11 bxc3 ♗e7 *(D)*

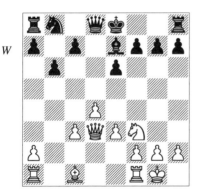

The opening stage is nearly over. White has an obvious advantage but now needs to form a plan. Soultanbéieff does not opt for the most natural option, 12 e4, followed by 13 ♗f4. Perhaps he felt that this would weaken d4 a little.

Still, he manages to find another highly enterprising idea.

12 ♘e5!?

Knights, which are short-range weapons, like to be located near the targets in the opponent's camp. But here the real idea is to free the f-pawn to advance.

12...0-0 13 f4!

Now the idea is clarified: the solid c3-d4-e3 pawn-structure will be maintained for the time being, while White will attack with his queen and rook on the f-file.

13...c5 14 f5 exf5 15 ♕xf5

Since the beginning of the game, Black has had a hard time finding a constructive game plan. Still, his position can be considered solid. In this position, Dubyna thinks that his main problem is caused by his undeveloped knight. A reasonable thought in itself, but tactics take priority over every other consideration, right?

15...♕d5? *(D)*

With the idea of preparing ...♘c6. Correct plan, wrong execution: this development can be prepared by 15...♕e8, which also supports the f7-pawn and avoids leaving any loose pieces. 15...♕c8 is also far more solid.

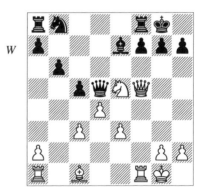

16 ♘g6!

A double attack with a knight-fork theme. Suddenly Black's queen and bishop (the two *loose pieces* at which the previous note hinted) are under attack.

16...♕b7

The only possibility to prolong the struggle. Instead, 16...♕d7 17 ♕xd7 ♘xd7 18 ♘xe7+ is winning for White, while 16...♕e6 17 ♕xe6 fxe6 18 ♘xe7+ ♔h8 19 ♖xf8# is even mate!

For 16...♕d6, we see that the problems with the f7-square don't even allow Black to play on an exchange down: 17 ♘xf8! and the knight cannot be touched because of ♕xf7+, followed by mate.

17 ♕d5!

The 'queen hunt' continues. An instructive example of the *overloading* theme.

17...♘c6

In desperation, Black seeks salvation by cutting the contact between the opposing queens. Unfortunately, this is a futile effort...

18 ♕xc6!

An elegant way to end this game: because 18...♕xc6 19 ♘xe7+ ♔h8 20 ♘xc6 gives White a decisive material advantage, Dubyna duly resigned.

1-0

When Everything Goes According to Plan

Game 25

Freeman – Mednis

New York 1955

King's Indian Defence

1 d4 ♘f6 2 c4 g6 3 ♘c3 ♗g7 *(D)*

The first steps of the *King's Indian Defence*. Instead, 3...d5 would carry the position to Grünfeld waters.

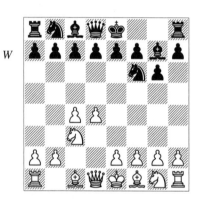

The King's Indian Defence is a counterattacking system, in which Black yields the centre to his opponent at an early stage of the game. Later on, Black will target White's structure with his fianchettoed bishop, supported by pawn advances such as ...c5 or ...e5. Both sides have a wide range of options, and this fact makes the King's Indian one of the most complex and deeply analysed opening systems in chess.

4 g3

In his turn, Freeman chooses to control the centre from a distance, just like his opponent.

Classical systems beginning with 4 e4 usually tend to create positions with a closed centre.

4...0-0 5 ♗g2 d6 6 ♘f3 ♘c6

The location of the queen's knight determines the further course of the game. The main alternative is 6...♘bd7, when Black normally attacks White's centre with ...e5. The text-move, however, supports Black's play against the d4-square in more direct fashion, while also provoking White to advance immediately with d5.

7 e4?!

This allows Black to create intense pressure against the d4-pawn. If White wishes to adopt this approach, he does better to castle and then play h3 (preventing ...♗g4) before playing e4.

7...♗g4 *(D)*

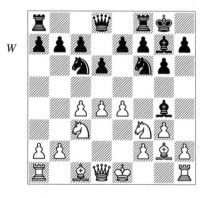

The consistent follow-up to Black's plan of piece-play against the pawn-centre.

8 h3

Freeman feels it is worth spending a tempo to force the g4-bishop to declare its intentions. By eliminating Black's bishop, White will enjoy the celebrated 'bishop-pair advantage', right? However, this is not a position where the bishop-pair will shine, whereas the black knights will prove highly nimble. 8 ♗e3, reinforcing d4, is a reasonable alternative.

8...♗xf3 9 ♗xf3 ♘d7!

Now it's the g7-bishop's turn to take aim at d4.

10 ♗e3

Oddly enough, 10 d5 ♘a5!? 11 ♗e2 ♘b6 gives White problems with his c4-pawn. Therefore, White does not yet want to change the character of the centre with a committal and irreversible step.

10...♘a5!?

It was possible to continue with the 'play against d4' strategy with 10...e5 11 d5 ♘d4 12 ♗g2 c5. After the text-move, however, the game revolves around the c4-square.

11 ♕a4 *(D)*

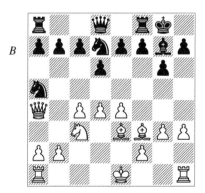

11...c5

The knight can maintain its presence on the edge due to this important pawn advance.

12 d5 a6!?

Black intends to seize the initiative on the queenside with ...b5.

13 ♗d2?!

Since the beginning of the game, White has played (at least seemingly) normal moves, yet still he faces serious problems. How can this

be possible? The answer to this question is pretty simple: while one can evaluate a single move as good or bad in itself, the harmony and coherence of the moves, plans and the ideas behind them are much more important. In our case, although Black has made some little adjustments, his consistent plan of putting pressure on White's centre was always there. In contrast, White's messy and unprincipled play has put him in a dim position, where he still has not managed to castle, and he has to fight with Black's various threats all the time.

13...♘e5 14 ♗e2 *(D)*

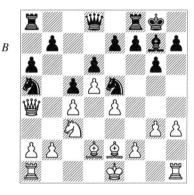

14...♘axc4!

It is very important to start the tactics before White has managed to castle. 12...a6 commenced Black's plan of seizing the initiative on the queenside, and now the real action begins.

15 ♗xc4 b5 16 ♗xb5 axb5 *(D)*

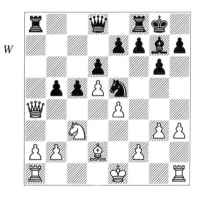

17 ♕c2

One might think: "OK, why not 17 ♕xb5?" Probably his opponent's play on the b-file scared

White off: 17...♘f3+ 18 ♔d1 (18 ♔e2 ♘d4+) 18...♖xd2 19 ♔xd2 ♖b8. After the text-move, owever, Black will accelerate his attack by gaining a tempo with his b-pawn.

17...b4 18 ♘d1 ♘f3+ 19 ♔f1 *(D)*

19 ♔e2 was out of the question because of the knight fork on d4. Do you think it is possible for White to run away from possible forking themes so easily?

beautiful opportunities. Mednis has calculated that his rook is taboo: 20 ♖xa2 b3! 21 ♕c1 (21 ♕xb3 is met by 21...♘xd2+) 21...bxa2 is winning for Black.

20 ♖b1 ♕a5

More reserves join the assault. We won't have to wait long to witness the queen's support in the attack!

21 ♔g2 b3! *(D)*

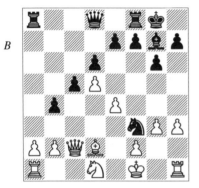

19...♖xa2!

A bolt from the blue! Although it is obvious that White is struggling, it requires a certain tactical vision not to miss such effective and

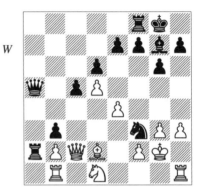

A *discovered attack* finishes the game in splendid fashion: 22 ♗xa5 bxc2 or 22 ♕xb3 ♘xd2.

0-1

Prince Urusov's Recipe

Game 26
Neishtadt – Gipslis
Latvia vs Russian Federation, Riga 1955
Bishop's Opening

1 e4 e5 2 ♗c4

With the white pieces, some players find it hard to get a tangible edge against solid systems such as the Petroff (1 e4 e5 2 ♘f3 ♘f6) or Berlin (1 e4 e5 2 ♘f3 ♘c6 3 ♗b5 ♘f6). Therefore, from time to time, we see them trying different openings, like the Centre Game, Vienna Game and, as in this example, the *Bishop's Opening*.

2...♘f6 3 d4!?

The *Urusov Gambit*. White embraces a rather aggressive attitude in the opening stage, directly targeting his opponent's centre with a pawn sacrifice.

3...♘xe4

Not the stiffest test of the validity of this enterprising system. After 3...exd4 4 ♘f3, the game can transpose to the Scotch Gambit with 4...♘c6. But in the 4...♘xe4 5 ♕xd4 variation, White would have to demonstrate the correctness of his sacrifice, with his temporary, but powerful, initiative.

4 dxe5

Suddenly, there appear tactical ideas based on the traditionally weak f7-square: ♕d5 and/or ♗xf7+.

4...♘c5

Consequently, Black takes his loose knight to a safer square.

5 ♘f3 ♗e7 6 ♗f4 ♘c6 7 ♘c3 ♘e6 8 ♗g3 *(D)*

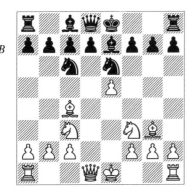

While the e5-pawn might turn into a burden in the long run, for the moment, it is precisely this pawn that restricts Black's development and gives White a space advantage.

8...0-0 9 ♕e2

White does not want to play cautiously by castling kingside. The slightly closed character of the centre makes a kingside attack more attractive, so queenside castling is both preferable and more consistent with his play so far.

9...f5?

This seemingly ambitious advance is actually not fast enough. Black will never find the required time to trap the g3-bishop.

10 0-0-0!? *(D)*

It should be mentioned that 10 exf6 ♗xf6 11 0-0-0 also works out well for White.

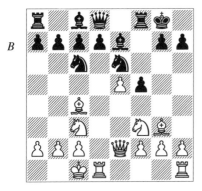

Thanks to the pin on the d-file, ♗xe6+ is now a serious threat.

10...♕e8

Unpinning the d7-pawn. But this idea will not be sufficient against White's constant threats.

11 ♘d5!

Now Neishtadt benefits from the pin of the e6-knight, and threatens ♘xc7.

11...♔h8 12 ♘f4

With his last two moves, White has transferred his knight to the kingside, where the real action will take place. In view of the next note, he might have considered preparing this move with 12 h4!? (which also provides a square for the g3-bishop).

12...a6?

Here, one might think of an interesting defensive idea: 12...g5!? (a rather radical measure in front of Black's own king) 13 ♘xe6 dxe6 with a somewhat unclear position. Probably Gipslis declined this option as it seemed a bit risky, but this was his best chance by far. As it is, he will face real difficulties when his planned queenside counterplay turns out to be slower than expected.

13 h4!

Preparing ♘g5.

13...♘a5 *(D)*

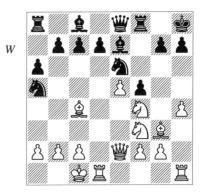

14 ♗xe6!

Giving up the strong bishop is not an easy decision to make. But as in most other gambit systems, maintaining the initiative is a key factor.

14...dxe6 15 ♘g5

As mentioned before, knights are most effective when they are located near the targets in the opponent's camp.

15...♗c5 *(D)*

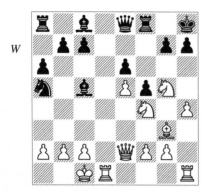

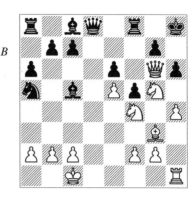

16 ♖d8!!

This outstanding move *deflects* Black's queen from her defensive task of controlling h5. While it was quite evident that White had good attacking prospects due to his many active pieces, such a beautiful rook sacrifice can only be considered as a gem!

16...♕xd8 17 ♕h5 h6

There's no other way to prevent the threat of ♕xh7#.

18 ♕g6! *(D)*

The queen is sneakily getting closer to her prey.

Black has no choice besides removing the white knight on g5, even though this results in the opening of the h-file.

18...hxg5 19 hxg5+ ♔g8 20 ♕h5

This is one of many winning options. White does not allow the black king to run away via f7. At the same time, he clears the way for the g6 advance.

20...♘c4 21 g6 ♕d2+ 22 ♔b1

As Black's pieces are too scattered to create any discomfort for White's king, the game is already over.

22...♘a3+ 23 bxa3 1-0

Lining Up on the Third Rank

Game 27

Nezhmetdinov – Kotkov

Russian Federation Ch, Krasnodar 1957

Ruy Lopez

1 e4 e5 2 ♘f3 ♘c6 3 ♗b5 ♘f6

This is the *Berlin Defence*, the main line of which is a complex queenless middlegame. But of course, White has other possibilities too.

4 0-0 ♘xe4 5 ♖e1

In 2000, the then World Chess Champion Kasparov met the challenger Kramnik for the world title. In that match, Kramnik resurrected this old line, which was at that point a rather neglected system. Facing this seemingly passive but very solid defence, Kasparov replied with the main line, 5 d4 ♘d6 6 ♗xc6 (after 6 dxe5

♘xb5 7 a4 ♘bd4 8 ♘xd4 ♘xd4 9 ♕xd4 d5 White can at most claim a very slight plus) 6...dxc6 (6...bxc6, followed by the transfer of the knight to b7, is also interesting, but far less solid) 7 dxe5 ♘f5 8 ♕xd8+ ♔xd8. At first glance this might look like a boring endgame position, but it can lead to a sharp and rich middlegames – after all, there are still many pieces left on the board and there is considerable imbalance in the position.

In our case, however, White opts for a line in which the queens stay on the board. Still, one should point out that it can be quite hard to achieve a tangible plus with the symmetrical pawn-structure that is about to arise.

5...♘d6 6 ♘xe5 ♗e7 *(D)*

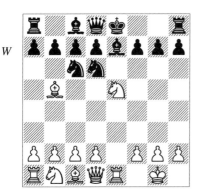

7 ♗d3!?

Most of the time, exchanging pieces tends to favour the side with a cramped position. A position tends to have a natural 'capacity', beyond which the pieces simply get in each other's way. On the other hand, a player with a space advantage prefers to have a lot of pieces to 'patrol' this vast domain and keep intruders out.

So if possible, it makes sense for the side with a space advantage to avoid unforced simplifications. Nezhmetdinov understands that the knight on d6 is the main factor in Black's space disadvantage, as it blocks the d7-pawn. The move chosen 'cuts out' this knight's squares. However, the bishop itself cuts an odd impression on d3: for the moment, it blocks the d2-pawn and therefore delays the development of the dark-squared bishop.

7...♘xe5 8 ♖xe5 0-0 9 ♘c3 ♗f6

Who would have predicted that this logical move, questioning the rook's presence on e5, was not the most accurate move? After witnessing the game continuation, it may be possible to claim that 9...c6 10 ♕f3 ♘e8! 11 b3 d5 was an easier path to equality. Yet at this moment it is hard to imagine that the bishop belongs on the a3-f8 diagonal.

10 ♖e3 g6 11 ♕f3 ♗g7 12 b3 ♘e8

To solve his development problems, Black is willing to retreat his pieces temporarily. But on the contrary, White has developed nearly all his forces.

13 ♗a3 d6 14 ♖ae1 *(D)*

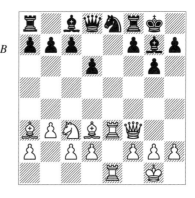

Very interesting chess: instead of trying to get an advantage by putting his pawns in the centre, White has lined up his pieces in front of them on the third rank. But this suffices for an edge because Black's pieces are mostly on their first rank.

14...♘f6 15 h3

Not permitting ...♗g4.

15...♘d7 *(D)*

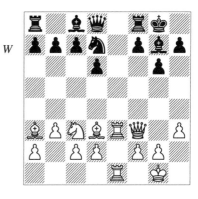

Black cannot find a decent plan against his opponent's extraordinary set-up, and embarks on some ineffective manoeuvres. His idea is to stop Nezhmetdinov's pressure along the e-file by playing ...♘e5. But White's natural reply prevents this plan.

16 ♘d5!

Forward!

16...f5?!

Before analysing the game continuation, we should find out why Black did not opt for 16...♘e5. White seizes a decisive initiative with the exchange sacrifice 17 ♖xe5! dxe5 (after 17...♗xe5? 18 ♖xe5! dxe5 19 ♗e7 the queen runs out of safe squares) 18 ♗e7 ♕d7 19 ♘f6+

♗xf6 20 ♕xf6 (20 ♗xf8 is also interesting) 20...♖e8 21 ♖xe5. After this long variation, White has the more active pieces and play on the dark squares, as well as an extra pawn.

We now return to 16...f5?! *(D)*:

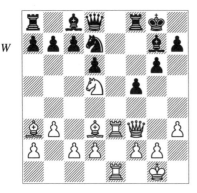

17 ♘xc7!

White lures the queen away from its main duty of controlling the back rank, while at the same time clearing the d5-square for the white queen. Taking into consideration Black's 'sleeping' pieces on the queenside, White's active forces and the recently weakened a2-g8 diagonal, it is no surprise that this sacrifice proves successful.

17...♕xc7 18 ♕d5+ ♔h8 19 ♖e8

The ♕f7 idea has turned into a serious threat.

19...♘f6 20 ♖xf8+ ♗xf8 21 ♗b2!

With its counterpart, albeit temporarily, leaving the long diagonal, White's dark-squared bishop finds a better square for itself.

21...♗g7 22 ♗c4!

Now 22...♘xd5? would allow 23 ♖e8#.

22...♗d7

Black, at last, finds a way to develop his light-squared bishop and partly resolve his back-rank problems. Why partly? Nezhmetdinov's instructive *coup de grâce* will answer this question best.

23 ♗xf6 ♗xf6 24 ♕f7 ♕d8? *(D)*

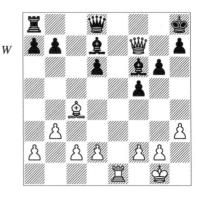

25 ♖e8+! 1-0

A Bolt from the Blue

Game 28

Gaisert – I. Zaitsev

USSR Team Ch, Moscow 1960

Tarrasch Defence

1 d4 d5 2 c4 e6 3 ♘c3 c5

The *Tarrasch Defence*. Against the Queen's Gambit, rather than forming a solid set-up by strengthening d5 with moves like 3...c6 or simple development, Black is ready to accept structural weaknesses in return for active piece-play.

4 cxd5 cxd4

The main line of the Tarrasch is 4...exd5 5 ♘f3 ♘c6, when material is level but Black is likely to get an isolated d-pawn.

The text-move is the *Hennig-Schara Gambit*. Black does not want to deal with the possible problems of an isolated pawn. With this ultra-aggressive approach, he is content to give up a pawn in return for generating early pressure on his opponent.

5 ♕xd4 ♘c6

Developing the pieces to effective squares with tempo lays the foundation for Black's active play.

6 ♕d1 exd5 7 ♕xd5 *(D)*

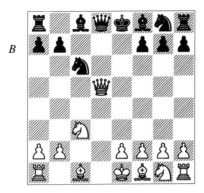

Three consecutive moves by the queen in the opening... Having seen quite a number of instructive miniatures, we are well aware that White will need to be careful over the next few moves.

7...♗d7

Black, on the other hand, prevents the exchange of queens (which would limit his attacking possibilities) with another developing move.

8 ♗g5

White normally plays more modestly with 8 ♘f3 ♘f6 9 ♕d1 (or 9 ♕b3!?), when it is a good deal harder for Black to prove that he has enough compensation for the pawn.

8...♘f6 9 ♗xf6

9 ♕d2 is seen more often. After the text-move, Black's queen joins the battle without losing a tempo, and this is quite important, as is the fact that White is liable to be vulnerable on the dark squares after giving up this bishop.

9...♕xf6 10 e3 0-0-0 *(D)*

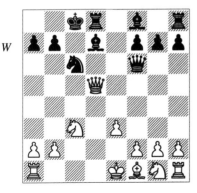

A wide open position, a king in the centre, and now ...0-0-0! Taking all these factors into

consideration, one can easily understand that here White's main task is to bring his king to safety.

11 ♕b3 ♗e6 12 ♕a4?

Why not 12 ♗c4, trying to swap the undeveloped bishop for its counterpart on e6? Perhaps Gaisert was dreaming of attacking the black king with ideas like ♗a6. In any case, White should have given priority to his king's safety.

12...♗b4

The threat of winning a pawn with ...♗xc3+ does not allow White to put his ♗a6 idea into practice.

13 ♖c1? *(D)*

White has fallen significantly behind his opponent in development, and now allows a deadly tactical blow.

The threat against c3 makes it hard for White to catch up in development; the only move is 13 ♘e2, but what would White's next step then be, even if he were allowed some peace and quiet? Not that he will be; after 13...♖d3 White is engaged in a desperate fight for survival.

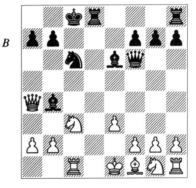

13...♖d2!!

We've seen some similar examples in our book, yet Zaitsev's move was a genuine bolt from the blue! There is no choice but to accept the offer, as ...♕xf2# is a deadly threat, and 14 ♘ge2 is met by 14...♖xb2.

14 ♔xd2 ♕xf2+

Black's idea is clear: in this open position, he will attack the 'centralized' white king. Still, Black must also act carefully, as even a tiny mistake in the calculation process of a king-hunt might turn the sacrifice into an unfounded speculative idea.

15 ♘e2 ♗f5

The first mission has been completed: the escape-route via c2 is now closed! How can White prevent Black's most dangerous threat, ...♖d8#?

16 ♕xb4

Gaisert desperately sets a trap: 16...♘xb4?? is met by 17 ♘e4+! and suddenly it is White who is winning! But of course, Black is not obliged to capture the queen and comply with White's intentions.

16...♖d8+! 17 ♕d4

There are no reasonable defensive resources left.

17...♘xd4 18 ♘b5+ ♘c6+ *(D)*

18...♘c2+ would finish the game a bit more quickly. But the text-move is more than sufficient.

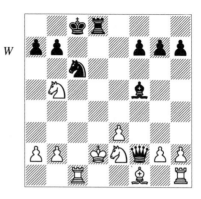

19 ♘d4 ♔b8 20 ♔d1 ♕xe3 0-1

An instructive example. In an open position, the problems caused by an uncastled king and backward development should never be underestimated, although it required considerable imagination by Black to take full advantage.

Let's Bring the King to the Centre!

Game 29
Taimanov – Polugaevsky
USSR Ch, Leningrad 1960
Queen's Gambit Accepted

1 d4 d5 2 c4 dxc4

We saw an example of the *Queen's Gambit Accepted* in Game 22.

3 ♘f3 ♘f6 4 ♕a4+!? *(D)*

As it is highly improbable that Black will be able to keep his c4-pawn in the long run, White usually opts for 4 e3 here. Maybe Taimanov chose this interesting move in order to disrupt the harmony in his opponent's camp.

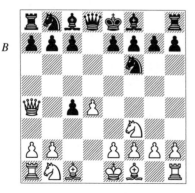

4...♘bd7

The game would transpose to a variation of the Slav Defence after 4...c6 5 ♕xc4 ♗f5.

5 ♘c3

The queen's presence on a4 is useful as it maintains a pin on the d7-knight. Therefore, instead of regaining his pawn immediately, White takes the opportunity to set up a well-supported pawn-centre.

5...e6 6 e4

The desired pawn-structure has been built. Black has to act quickly, so as not to fall into a passive position without any prospects.

6...c5

This is the only effective way to challenge White's central pawn duo.

7 d5 exd5 8 e5!

This is far more effective than acquiring a passed pawn with 8 exd5 followed by ♗xc4. Although passed pawns can prove important trumps in the long term, this option is not especially promising for White. The position would then be stabilized, reducing White's prospects of seizing the initiative. The passed d5-pawn is easily blockaded by a bishop (or at some point a knight) on d6, and will not only pose Black little threat, but may even prove a useful 'shield', protecting the blockading piece from frontal attack along the d-file. Therefore White continues with more forcing play.

8...d4?

Moving the knight from f6 was highly unappealing due to ♘xd5. However, many years later a better approach was demonstrated by the 12th World Champion, Anatoly Karpov: 8...b5!? 9 ♕xb5 (9 ♘xb5 would give Black's knight some mobility: 9...♘e4) 9...♖b8 10 ♕a4! (the pin must be preserved; otherwise the black pieces would suddenly join the battle) 10...d4 11 exf6 dxc3 12 ♗xc4 ♖b4! (12...cxb2? loses to 13 ♗xf7+!). With this last move, Black sows enough confusion amongst White's attacking forces to ensure his king's safety.

However, Polugaevsky, one of the best-prepared grandmasters of his time, did not have the benefit of having studied this position extensively at home, and decided to answer the threat with the most natural move.

9 exf6 dxc3 10 ♗xc4! *(D)*

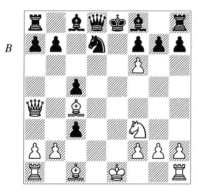

The bishop joins the fight with great effect. The tension caused by the c3- and f6-pawns gives the position an unusual twist and this demands precise calculation from both players. Taimanov is aware that his f6-pawn plays an important role by controlling e7, and thereby stopping ideas like ...♕e7+. All in all, development has once again the priority!

10...♕xf6

The discomforting pawn must be eliminated. But this capture allows White's forces to join the battle with gain of time.

11 ♗g5 ♕c6 *(D)*

Of course, 11...cxb2? loses to 12 ♗xf6.

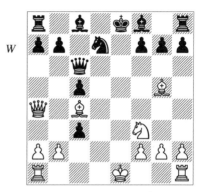

Black anticipates that an exchange of queens will lessen the force of his opponent's attack.

12 0-0-0!!

It's because of moves like this that chess is such a beautiful game! In order to accelerate his attack on the open central files, Taimanov is ready to sacrifice his queen.

12...cxb2+

What happens if Black accepts this 'generous' offer? 12...♕xa4 13 ♖he1+ ♗e7 14 ♖xe7+ ♔f8 (14...♔d8 15 ♖exd7++ ♔e8 16 ♖d8#) 15 ♖xf7+ ♔g8 16 ♖fxd7+ ♕xc4 17 ♖d8+ ♔f7 18 ♘e5+ ♔e6 19 ♘xc4. Even if this is a very long sequence of moves, actually it is not that hard to calculate, as the line is more or less forced.

With the text-move, at least, Black wanted White to determine his king's position.

13 ♔xb2

In fact, White has the luxury of a choice, but in situations like this, it is often safer to hide the king in front of the pawn. But both 13 ♔xb2 and 13 ♔b1 win comfortably in this instance.

13...♗e7 14 ♖he1 f6

The only way to stop ♖xe7+. But White still has many ways to fuel his initiative.

15 ♗b5 ♕b6 16 ♔c1

Taimanov will resume his attack once the bishop is freed from the pin. Although White's king seems more exposed than its counterpart, Black lacks forces that could target it.

16...fxg5

As there is no way to save the pinned knight on d7, Black has no choice but to capture the g5-bishop.

17 &xd7+ &f8 (D)

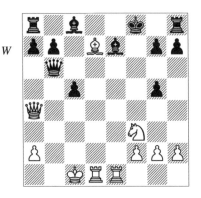

18 ♖xe7!

With the enemy forces so scattered and the king so vulnerable, it is natural to seek a sacrificial breakthrough. Taimanov launches a king-hunt that denies his opponent any chance to take even a breath of fresh air.

18...&xe7 19 ♛e4+ &d8 20 &f5+ &c7 21 ♛e5+ &c6 22 ♖d6+ &b5

22...&c7 23 ♖d7++ &c6 24 ♘d4+! (the fifth rank is cleared with the help of this sacrifice) 24...cxd4 25 ♛d5# was a possible scenario.

23 ♛b2+ 1-0

Polugaevsky decided that he had seen enough. 23...&a5 24 ♛a3+ &b5 25 ♘d4+! (this time, the knight is sacrificed so as not to allow ...c4) 25...cxd4 26 &d3# would be a fitting end to this highly instructive battle.

Fischer's Provocation

Game 30
Letelier – Fischer
Leipzig Olympiad 1960
King's Indian Defence

1 d4 ♘f6 2 c4 g6 3 ♘c3 &g7 4 e4 0-0!? (D)

Black normally plays 4...d6 and then castles.

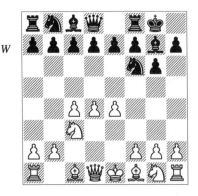

In the *King's Indian Defence* (KID), Black allows his opponent to set up a big pawn-centre in the opening. This in itself is enough to make the KID a highly provocative defence. But normally Black doesn't also allow White

to play e5 so easily. From time to time, when great players face lesser opponents, they use unconventional approaches, even if objectively they may not be the best choice. The aim is to create an unbalanced position where the better player will generally emerge on top. In this case, the 11th World Champion might have wanted to avoid his opponent's preparation.

5 e5

Quite a committal move, since pawns cannot move backwards. From now on, White has to prove that his space advantage is more important than all the other elements in the position. He could instead have played a normal developing move (such as 5 ♘f3), as Black is unlikely to find a better move than 5...d6, when the play reverts to normal King's Indian channels.

5...♘e8 6 f4

Supporting his e5-pawn, which will be a target for Black's forces very soon. Still, White's highly ambitious play has some minuses like over-expansion and delaying the development of the minor pieces. White could instead develop more modestly (e.g., 6 ♘f3), and answer Black's ...d6 advance with exd6. This is not only safer, but may be a better objective attempt to cast some doubt on Black's ultra-provocative play.

6...d6

Fischer initiates his counterplay by increasing the pressure on e5.

7 ♗e3 c5!

Undermining the base of the pawn-chain. The handling of pawn-chains is a very important strategic issue, which Nimzowitsch discussed at length in his writings. Fischer seeks to punish his opponent's many pawn moves by opening (or ideally destroying) the centre.

8 dxc5 ♘c6! *(D)*

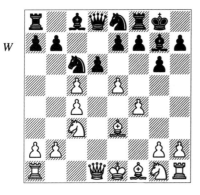

Maximizing the pressure on e5. White needs to keep the lines closed as long as possible.

9 cxd6 exd6 10 ♘e4

As an exchange of queens is unfavourable for Black, the e5-pawn should not be captured yet. Letelier is aiming to improve his knight's position, but it would probably have been better to strengthen e5 with the developing move 10 ♘f3.

10...♗f5

It is important to challenge the knight's central location, even at the cost of a tempo.

11 ♘g3

Although 11 ♘xd6 ♘xd6 12 ♕xd6 ♕xd6 13 exd6 brings about many exchanges, Black's remaining pieces would be very active after 13...♗xb2 followed by 14...♘b4.

11...♗e6 12 ♘f3 ♕c7

An all-out attack on the e5-pawn! A plan can only be successful if the pieces collectively support and serve its main idea.

13 ♕b1?!

White is now well aware that it's not possible to keep the e-file closed any more. Therefore, in an attempt to neutralize Black's pressure, Letelier is more than ready to give up his material advantage. Still, there is an important tactical flaw in this seemingly plausible plan.

13...dxe5 14 f5 *(D)*

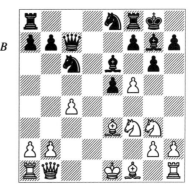

Now White's idea is clear: he will gain a tempo by attacking the bishop, while at the same time keeping the e-file closed.

14...e4!

After this unexpected advance, the tension on the board is rising. Opening up the position is obviously favourable for Black, as he is better developed.

15 fxe6

The f5-pawn cannot be captured after 15 ♕xe4 gxf5, as Black wins a piece following 16 ♘xf5? ♕a5+.

15...exf3 16 gxf3 f5!

A classy move. Of course, it was also possible to continue with 16...fxe6, but if there is a choice, connecting the pawns is certainly better.

17 f4

The pawn fork is prevented, but this time the e4-square has been weakened.

17...♘f6 18 ♗e2 ♖fe8

At last, the e-file will be opened after the removal of the pawn. In his turn, White immediately takes preventive measures to meet his opponent's deadly plan.

19 ♔f2 ♖xe6 20 ♖e1 ♖ae8

Now that this rook has joined the game, all the ingredients are ready for Black's final assault.

21 ♗f3 *(D)*

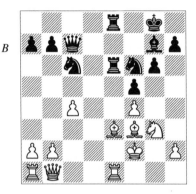

The bishop is protected, and control over the key e4-square has been strengthened. Still, all these considerations will prove to be insufficient after Fischer's upcoming sacrifices.

21...♖xe3!

Actually this first shot, aiming to pull White's king to the centre, is not that surprising.

22 ♖xe3 ♖xe3 23 ♔xe3 *(D)*

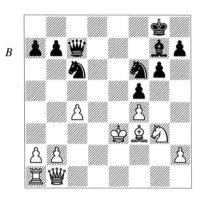

23...♕xf4+!

But this gigantic blow was unexpected.

0-1

Letelier rightfully resigns, as it's checkmate after 24 ♔xf4 ♗h6#, and loss is inevitable following 24 ♔f2 ♘g4+ 25 ♔g2 ♘e3+ 26 ♔f2 ♘d4 27 ♕h1 ♘g4+.

Mobilizing the Pawns

Game 31

Bronstein – Geller

USSR Ch, Moscow 1961

Nimzo-Indian Defence

1 d4 ♘f6 2 c4 e6 3 ♘c3 ♗b4

The *Nimzo-Indian Defence*. 'Hypermoderns', such as Réti and Nimzowitsch, did not embrace the classical preference for controlling the centre by occupying the squares with pawns. Instead, they claimed that when talking about controlling the centre, one has to mean the *squares*, not necessarily the pawns. Usually in 'modern' defences, such as the Nimzo-Indian, Black intends to control the centre with his minor pieces from a distance.

4 a3!?

Why spend a tempo forcing the bishop to exchange on c3, when in many lines it is quite willing to do so without being directly provoked? The answer is simple: White wishes to

clarify the situation so that he can devote all his energy to acquiring and mobilizing a powerful pawn-mass in the centre.

4...♗xc3+ 5 bxc3 0-0 6 f3 *(D)*

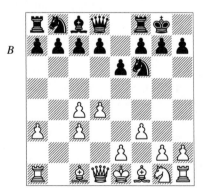

It's hard to assess which side is playing in a more modern fashion. To achieve an advantageous position, Bronstein thinks that the e4 advance is a must. Therefore, he doesn't hesitate to prepare this advance, even if it delays White's natural development.

6...d5

Of course, Black will not let his opponent put his plan into practice so easily. From now on, the battle will revolve around the e4 advance and its prevention.

7 cxd5 exd5 8 e3 ♗f5 9 ♘e2 *(D)*

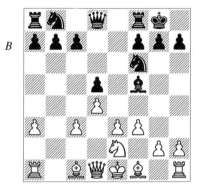

How can White hope to achieve a good position when he has been so slow to develop? We might liken the situation to kinetic and potential energy. While Black has been generating kinetic energy (fast development), White has been building up potential energy: a flexible pawn-mass in the centre and on the kingside, like an arrow about to leave the bow. Although White's king is still in the centre, and his bishops are yet to be developed, Black lacks concrete targets.

9...♘bd7 10 ♘f4

The knight's location has an important role over the course of the game. Alternatively, 10 ♘g3 would win a tempo by attacking the bishop. But then the important g4 advance would not be possible, because the knight is blocking it.

10...c5

Hindering the e4 advance once again: because of the pressure on d4, it's not possible to play 11 e4 yet.

11 ♗d3

The exchange of bishops deprives White of an important attacking weapon, but kingside development could not be delayed any longer.

Besides, the black bishop was well-placed and potentially an excellent defender.

11...♗xd3 12 ♕xd3 ♖e8 13 0-0 *(D)*

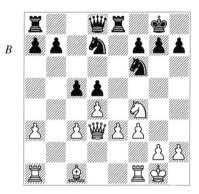

13...♖c8 14 ♖b1

Bronstein wants to put all his pieces on their ideal squares before taking any committal action. The aim is to leave Black's pieces in passive positions, with only defensive prospects.

14...♕a5!?

With this interesting idea, Black foresees that White's rook can be cut off if it captures the b7-pawn. Against 14...b6, the a4-a5 advance seems like a plausible plan for White.

15 ♖xb7 ♘b6 *(D)*

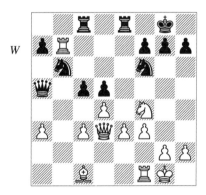

Black has sprung his trap, but White does not appear unduly troubled...

16 g4!

Although this is (at least partly) an open position, it is not easy to shake White's stance in the centre. This makes it is possible for White to play on the wing without fearing an immediate central counterblow. White wants to harass Black's knight with g5, and thereby weaken

Black's hold on d5, not to mention attacking chances on the kingside...

16...h6

It was obvious that White's planned advance will not be prevented after his natural reply, but Geller probably wanted to provoke his opponent to weaken his own king a little more.

17 h4 *(D)*

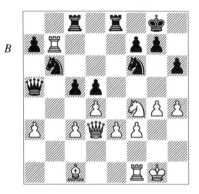

17...cxd4?!

With this dubious decision, Black had missed White's upcoming *zwischenzug* (in-between move). We shall see the outcome of this mistake in the game continuation, but now let's analyse an interesting alternative: 17...c4!? (usually such advances tend to favour White, as the tension on d4 has been released, but here there are some 'cunning ideas' regarding the rook on b7) 18 ♕f5 ♕a6 19 ♖xf7 (the rook has nowhere else to go) 19...♔xf7 20 g5 ♖c6! (Black seeks to punish White for weakening his king position

with the g5 and h4 pawn advances) 21 ♕g6+ ♔f8 22 gxh6!? (much better than 22 gxf6 ♖xf6) 22...gxh6 23 e4! (finally bringing the dark-squared bishop into the game). It is very hard to evaluate the final position.

Now, let's return to the game.

18 g5!

Instead of taking back his pawn, White accelerates his own attack.

18...dxe3

18...♖xc3 was an option worth considering, but still it fails against 19 ♗d2!: 19...♖xd3 20 ♗xa5 ♖dxe3 21 ♗xb6 axb6 22 gxf6 and White wins.

19 gxf6 ♖xc3? *(D)*

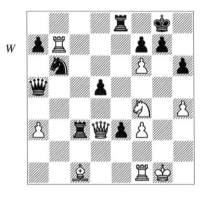

This final mistake in an already tough position allows White to finish the game elegantly.

20 ♕g6! 1-0

It is checkmate after 20...fxg6 21 ♖xg7+ ♔f8 (or 21...♔h8) 22 ♘xg6#.

In the Footsteps of Captain Evans

Game 32
Fischer – Fine
New York (offhand game) 1963
Evans Gambit

1 e4 e5 2 ♘f3 ♘c6 3 ♗c4 ♗c5 4 b4

We've already seen an example of the *Evans Gambit* in Game 1 of this book. In this opening, White does not hesitate to sacrifice a pawn or two in order to achieve a significant lead in development and/or a strong centre.

4...♗xb4 5 c3 ♗a5

Here 5...♗c5 and even 5...♗e7 are playable alternatives for Black. Apparently, Fine wishes to keep the pin on the a5-e1 diagonal, and thereby to prevent White from forming a strong centre with pawns on d4 and e4.

6 d4 exd4

After 6...d6, 7 0-0 ♗b6 transposes to Lasker's way of dealing with the Evans Gambit, while 7 ♕b3 ♕d7 8 dxe5 ♗b6 is another story.

7 0-0 *(D)*

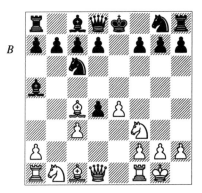

7...dxc3?!

But this capture is simply too greedy. It is better for Black to continue with his development: 7...♘ge7 8 ♘g5 d5 (White wins after 8...0-0? 9 ♕h5) 9 exd5 ♘e5 10 ♕xd4. Even if this is a complicated variation, it would not allow White to acquire the initiative as easily as in the game.

Now we'll witness White's forces swiftly joining the attack.

8 ♕b3

The f7-pawn has turned into a real target for White's pieces, after Fine has delayed his kingside development.

8...♕e7?

A better way to meet the threat was 8...♕f6. Although White would have some pressure after 9 e5 (9 ♗g5!? is also interesting) 9...♕g6 10 ♘xc3 ♘ge7 11 ♗a3 0-0 12 ♘e2 (with the idea of ♘f4, harassing the queen), it is too early to talk about a concrete advantage.

9 ♘xc3

At face value, this is a hard position to evaluate: do you think Black's material advantage is sufficient to neutralize White's pressure? It is not easy to give a definitive answer to this question, but at least in practice, Black faces a tough fight for survival.

9...♘f6?! *(D)*

A few moves ago, Black could have developed his pieces in relative normal fashion, but

he did not. Now, however, at the most untimely moment, he brings out this knight in such a way that White can force open lines and launch a direct attack on the black king.

It is not easy to find a viable line for Black, but 9...♗xc3 10 ♕xc3 ♘f6 may avoid an immediate collapse.

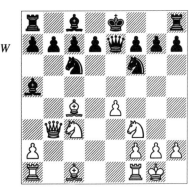

10 ♘d5!

As we've already mentioned a number of times, the initiative can only be sustained with forcing moves. Here, while attacking Black's queen, Fischer is mainly aiming to open the e-file.

10...♘xd5

Against the capture 10...♕xe4, White's reply 11 ♘g5 would turn attention to f7 once again (11 ♗g5 is also strong).

11 exd5 ♘e5

11...♘d8 is not possible, as after 12 ♗a3! d6 13 ♕b5+ Black's loose a5-bishop drops off.

12 ♘xe5 ♕xe5 13 ♗b2 *(D)*

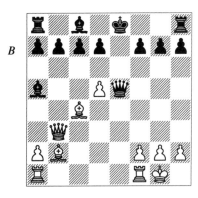

Now it's simple to evaluate the position. White has completed his development, and with his forcing moves he does not allow Black even to breathe. The upcoming attack along the e-file will decide matters very soon.

13...♕g5 14 h4!

This powerful move aims to deflect the queen from her defensive duty over g7. 14 ♕a3 was another strong option: White wins after the continuation 14...♗b6 15 ♗xg7! followed by ♖ae1+.

14...♕xh4

14...♕g4 cannot ease Black's suffering: 15 ♖fe1+! ♗xe1 16 ♖xe1+ ♔d8 (16...♔f8 loses to 17 ♕e3) 17 ♕e3 ♕xh4 (the only way to prevent checkmate on e7) 18 g3 and White wins as the queen has no squares.

15 ♗xg7

This capture is more than just a pawn-grab: the black king's escape-route via f8 is removed, and at the same time f6 has been prepared as a new attacking outpost.

15...♖g8 16 ♖fe1+ ♔d8 *(D)*

16...♗xe1 17 ♖xe1+ would be no different, as here the only valid consideration is checkmate, rather than material!

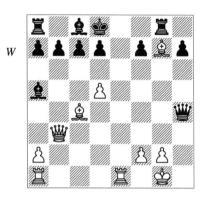

17 ♕g3! 1-0

A very nice example of *overloading*. Black's queen does not have any safe squares between d8 and h4, and must abandon her control over f6. It is checkmate after 17...♕xg3 18 ♗f6#.

Recalling an instructive game, a chess friend of mine urged me to analyse a very similar attacking example. A hundred years earlier, a very similar motif occurred in the following game:

A Similar Motif:

Linden – Maczuski
Paris 1863
Position after 11...♔e8-d8

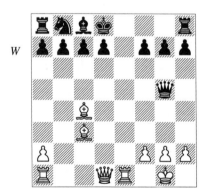

In this battle, Linden has sacrificed three pawns in his beloved *Danish Gambit* (1 e4 e5 2 d4 exd4 3 c3). In return, he has acquired a

distinct lead in development. Also, Black's king is stuck in the middle. As these are temporary advantages, it's time for White to strike with forcing moves.

12 f4!?

This fourth pawn sacrifice deflects the queen from her duty of defending g7. 12 h4 is also strong.

12...♕xf4 13 ♗xg7 ♖g8

Let's see what would have happened after 13...♖e8: 14 ♖xe8+ ♔xe8 15 ♕e2+ ♔d8 16 ♖e1 (threatening moves all along) 16...c6 17 ♕e7+ ♔c7 18 ♗e5+, winning the queen (Blatny).

14 ♕g4!

This fantastic strike reminds us of Fischer's beautiful finishing touch, 17 ♕g3!.

14...♕d6

The queen was taboo: 14...♕xg4 15 ♗f6#. All Black can do is prolong the hopeless struggle a little.

15 ♗f6+ 1-0

After 15...♖xf6, the brutal 16 ♕xg8# is curtains. Chess is a game of similarities, don't you agree?

A Memorable Blockading Tactic

Game 33
Fischer – Benko
USA Ch, New York 1963/4
Pirc Defence

1 e4 g6 2 d4 ♗g7 3 ♘c3 d6 4 f4 ♘f6 (D)

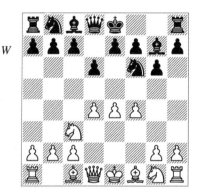

W

With Black's last move, the game has transposed from a Modern Defence (1 e4 g6) to a line of the Pirc Defence (which usually begins 1 e4 d6 2 d4 ♘f6).

The Pirc is similar to the King's Indian Defence, in that Black yields the centre to his opponent, and plans to attack White's central structure with timely pawn advances, supported by the fianchettoed bishop. Both sides base their play on different trumps, so a truly unbalanced position emerges right from the beginning of the game.

The Austrian Attack (4 f4) is one of the most ambitious and aggressive options against both the Pirc and Modern Defences. White's central structure is now even broader, and from now on the central e5 advance will be a highly pertinent idea.

5 ♘f3 0-0 6 ♗d3 ♗g4

As the light-squared bishop's ideal square has not been clarified yet, Black usually prefers to develop the queen's knight with 6...♘a6 or 6...♘c6. Benko, however, has other ideas: feeling that this bishop might have a hard time finding a decent square in the future, he opts for voluntarily exchanging it for one of White's knights.

7 h3 ♗xf3 8 ♕xf3 ♘c6

Black can develop his knight without worrying about the e5 advance, as the d4-pawn is hanging at the moment.

9 ♗e3 e5 (D)

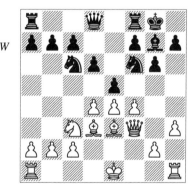

W

It seems like Black has more or less achieved his goals: he has completed his development, and at the same time prevented White's main idea, i.e. the e5 advance. Still, White is the one who will decide the further course of the game, as he has a more dominant voice over e5. After Fischer's decision, the f-file will be half-open, and the black bishop that could put pressure on the centre is blocked by its own pawn on the long diagonal.

10 dxe5 dxe5 11 f5

The centre, which was the focal point of tension just a couple of moves ago, has been stabilized. Black has to adjust his plan to the recent change in circumstances.

11...gxf5?!

Spoiling the pawn-structure, but why? Black should not be playing like 'Pollyanna': expecting White to reply with 12 exf5?! is just unrealistic. Although he would be a pawn down, Black has a great game after 12...e4! 13 ♘xe4 ♘xe4 14 ♗xe4 ♖e8. But White does not have to go in for this.

As a better option for Black, it is possible to consider 11...♘d4, followed by advancing the pawns on the queenside.

12 ♕xf5!

There is no need to cooperate with the opponent's desires.

12...♘d4 13 ♕f2 ♘e8

It's hard to suggest a constructive plan for Black. Benko tries to continue with manoeuvres that do not offer his opponent any more targets.

14 0-0 (D)

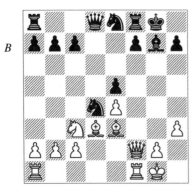

White has delayed castling for a long time, and actually this has tied Black's hands to some extent, because he couldn't commit to counterplay on one wing while the white king could easily sidestep by going the other way. Fischer once again chooses an option that will not give Benko even a tiny chance to become active.

14...♘d6 15 ♕g3

15 ♖ad1 was a very natural alternative. Here, however, White initiates a highly interesting strategy, with his queen heading towards the

kingside as a pioneer attacking force. The first threat is to benefit from the pin with ♗h6.

15...♔h8 16 ♕g4!?

Preventing ...f5. Here, Fischer's other idea was to eye the h7-square with 17 ♕h5. This way, checkmate ideas might appear after White removes the strong knight on d4 and follows up with e5.

16...c6

Restraining the c3-knight seems reasonable.

17 ♕h5 ♕e8? (D)

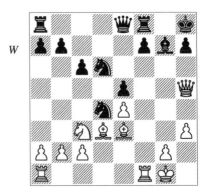

A grave mistake, since the concrete idea on which it is based does not work. Black is aiming to answer his opponent's above-mentioned plan 18 ♗xd4 exd4 19 e5 with 19...f5!. Can you spot the very important tactical flaw?

18 ♗xd4!

Apparently, Fischer disagrees with Benko's opinion.

18...exd4 19 ♖f6!! (D)

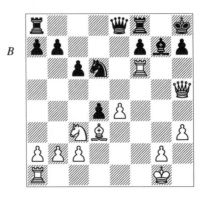

A magnificent idea! Sometimes a chess battle hinges on a way for one player to prevent a key point of his opponent's plan. White blocks the f7-pawn, so that it won't be able to move to f5 to prevent White's checkmate ideas.

19...♔g8

The rook was taboo: after 19...♗xf6 20 e5, mate on h7 is inevitable.

20 e5!

Now White continues with his original plan. Releasing the blockade with 20 ♖xd6? would be inconsistent: after 20...dxc3 21 e5, Black can now play 21...f5!.

20...h6

There's nothing else to be done against the threat of mate at h7.

21 ♘e2

After the knight heads to a safe square, celebrations can begin! In addition to the ongoing checkmate idea (21...♗xf6 22 ♕xh6), Black's paralysed d6-knight is decisive (21...♘b5 22 ♕f5).

1-0

The Wrong Strategy against Tal

Game 34

Tal – Tringov

Amsterdam Interzonal 1964

Modern Defence

1 e4 g6

This is the *Modern Defence*, or rather one form of it, since this opening is characterized by Black playing 1...g6 and ...♗g7 against more or less any opening moves by White.

2 d4 ♗g7 3 ♘c3 d6 4 ♘f3 c6

Black's approach is quite similar to the Pirc Defence, but with an important difference: here, Black delays ...♘f6 for some time, or even plays the knight to a different square altogether. With such a move-order, Black refrains from blocking his fianchettoed bishop, so that it will be easier to soften up White's centre with ...e5 or ...c5 advances. Also, don't forget the fact that a knight on f6 might be harassed by an early e5 advance.

Nowadays, another popular approach for Black is a kind of double fianchetto system, after queenside expansion with ...a6 followed by ...b5.

5 ♗g5!?

An odd-looking, provocative move: White prepares to meet 5...♘f6 with 6 ♕d2, intending ♗h6, while preventing this idea by 5...h6 might turn this pawn into a target after 6 ♗e3, with ♕d2 to follow.

5...♕b6 (D)

Black initiates his plan of eyeing the b2- and d4-pawns simultaneously. Why ...♘f6 has been delayed is now clear.

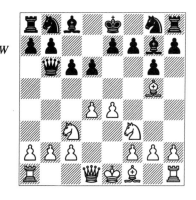

6 ♕d2!

A brave decision: White wishes to seize a tangible advantage in development, and does not want to spend any time protecting b2.

6...♕xb2

Challenge gladly accepted!

7 ♖b1 ♕a3 8 ♗c4

Thanks to his 'pawn-hunting' approach, Tringov has already delayed his development significantly. From now on, he must be very careful not to fall victim to White's tactical blows. Unfortunately, he made a grave mistake on his first move after the forced sequence.

8...♕a5?

One might instinctively feel that the queen's presence in White's camp places it in danger and that it therefore makes sense to retreat it to a safe location. But this is actually a typical error, and it allows White to establish very firm compensation. It is often the case that after a pawn-grab the queen should stay in contact with the enemy camp, where it causes considerable disruption. Of course, precise calculation is needed to make sure the queen isn't in excessive danger of actually being trapped.

Black should have prioritized development; 8...♘f6 seems more logical. Let's check a forcing variation: 9 e5 dxe5 10 dxe5 ♘fd7 11 ♖b3 (11 e6 cannot be played yet, since the c3-knight and the queen would be hanging) 11...♕c5! (D).

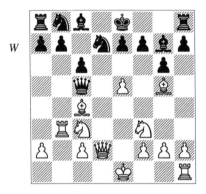

Now, it's not possible to continue the attack by normal means, as the c4-bishop is *en prise*. If White tries to expose Black's king with 12 ♗xf7+! ♔xf7 13 e6+, then after the further moves 13...♔g8! (13...♔xe6 14 ♗e3 seems risky for Black) 14 exd7 ♘xd7 15 0-0 h6! 16 ♗f4 (Black has no significant problems after 16 ♗e3 ♕d6) 16...♔h7 the problems caused by Black's disorganized pieces have been solved.

Throughout the book, I have generally refrained from giving complex variations. However, the handling of every position differs from others, according to their character. Black has shown great bravery by grabbing the b2-pawn, but he had to pursue his approach by relying on concrete calculations, rather than general considerations.

9 0-0 e6 (D)

This is an artificial development plan, but Black had little choice at this point. Black is rightfully worried about the effect of the c4-bishop, and postpones the natural plan of ...♘f6

followed by ...0-0 in view of the following line: 9...♘f6? 10 e5 (after Black has played so many queen moves, the conditions are right for this advance) 10...dxe5 11 dxe5 ♘fd7 12 ♗xe7! and White wins. Note that the queen falls after 12...♔xe7 13 ♘d5+, emphasizing the point that the retreat to 'safety' was illusory. If the opponent firmly possesses the initiative, then nothing is safe.

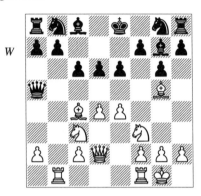

10 ♖fe1 a6

Black has no way to castle his king into safety; for instance, 10...♘e7 11 ♗xe7 ♔xe7 12 ♘d5+ and White wins.

11 ♗f4 e5?

In his book *Mastering Opening Strategy*, Johan Hellsten summarizes the inaccuracy of this pawn advance as follows: "When you are behind in development, the more closed the position the better for you, so don't even think about opening it! After that, it will be much easier for the opponent to make use of his more active pieces." A great piece of advice!

12 dxe5 dxe5 13 ♕d6! (D)

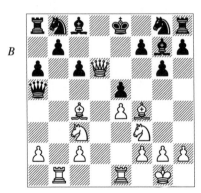

Once the d-file has been opened, the penetration by the queen is an obvious idea. But are all the circumstances right? Let's look once more at some concrete variations: 13...♕d8? 14 ♗xf7+!; 13...exf4 14 ♘d5!!. In the first variation we see the effect of the a2-g8 diagonal, and in the second variation the e-file. Tringov thinks that he has nothing better than grabbing material and decides to capture the hanging knight.

13...♕xc3 14 ♖ed1 ♘d7

Desperately trying to keep lines closed.

15 ♗xf7+!

After the exposure of his king, Black will be helpless.

15...♔xf7 *(D)*

15...♔d8 16 ♘g5 ♕c4 17 ♖d5! and White wins.

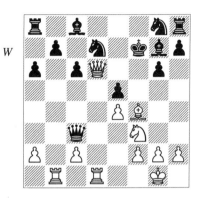

16 ♘g5+ ♔e8 17 ♕e6+ 1-0

The Penalty for a Single Bad Move

Game 35

Geller – Portisch

Moscow 1967

Ruy Lopez

1 e4 e5 2 ♘f3 ♘c6 3 ♗b5

Once again, the *Ruy Lopez*.

3...a6 4 ♗a4 ♘f6 5 0-0 ♗e7 6 ♖e1 b5

The move 6 ♖e1 provided firm support to the e4-pawn, so finally Black has to prevent the ♗xc6 idea, so as not to lose his e5-pawn.

7 ♗b3 d6 8 c3 0-0 9 h3

This is one of the most popular positions in the whole of chess history. White wishes to build a strong pawn-centre with d4, but first prevents ...♗g4. If White plays 9 d4 directly, Black can put pressure on d4 by pinning the knight with 9...♗g4.

9...h6

The *Smyslov Variation*. Here, on the other hand, ...h6 has not been played to support the centre. Instead, this little pawn move prepares a regrouping with ...♖e8 and ...♗f8, by preventing White's probable reply, ♘g5.

10 d4 ♖e8 11 ♘bd2

The Ruy Lopez provides some excellent examples of a general opening concept: developing first of all those pieces whose ideal positions have already been clarified. That's why the queen's knight now makes three moves before the c1-bishop has made even a single move: the knight heads off to a journey to g3 (or e3), where it might be most effective, leaving the bishop development for later.

11...♗f8 *(D)*

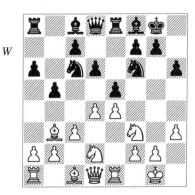

12 ♘f1 ♗b7 13 ♘g3

We see that both sides have developed their pieces in a logical manner. It is quite typical for the Closed Ruy Lopez that so far not even a single pawn has been exchanged.

Now, Black can continue by building an ideal defensive set-up with 13...g6, followed by ...♗g7. But Portisch impatiently wants to connect his rooks, and commits a significant mistake.

13...♕d7?!

Weaknesses in the enemy's camp are rarely handed to you on a silver platter. Most of the time, these secret opportunities need to be created, or at least exposed. In this specific case, Geller can only benefit from the black queen's insecure position by making a sequence of accurate moves.

14 dxe5 dxe5 *(D)*

After 14...♘xe5 15 ♘xe5 dxe5 16 ♕f3, threats such as ♗xh6 and ♘f5 would make the position advantageous for White.

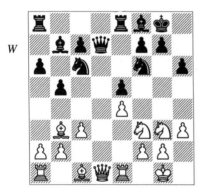

15 ♘h5!

Overloading the f6-knight leads at least to the destruction of Black's kingside pawn-structure. Of course, the white knight is 'untouchable': 15...♘xh5?? 16 ♕xd7.

15...♕e7?!

15...♕xd1 16 ♘xf6+ gxf6 17 ♖xd1 was the lesser evil for Black. Looking at his decision, one might claim that Portisch was still unaware of the upcoming problems. Ignorance is bliss, but not all the time.

16 ♘h4!

A typical manoeuvre in such structures. The knight sets its eyes on both f5 and g6.

16...♘xh5

Seeking salvation by removing one of the knights on the kingside. But this capture leads

to a different form of attack, in which White's queen also participates.

17 ♕xh5 ♘a5? *(D)*

Going into full defensive mode with 17...♘d8 was the only way to resist.

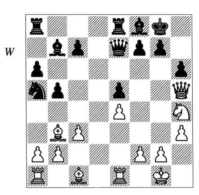

As Black doesn't have a counterpart to the 'Lopez bishop' on the a2-g8 diagonal, he reasonably aims to repel this important force. If White now cooperates by playing 18 ♗c2, Black can calmly play 18...g6 and release the pressure almost completely.

But it's Geller's turn, and he find a strong reply that denies Black time to eliminate the b3-bishop.

18 ♗g5!

The dark-squared bishop joins the attack with great impact, especially as it enables the 'sleeping' rook on a1 to take part in the action.

18...♕d7

The bishop was taboo: 18...♕xg5? 19 ♕xf7+ ♔h7 20 ♕g8# or 18...hxg5? 19 ♘g6! followed by 20 ♕h8# (once again, note the effect of the Lopez bishop!).

19 ♖ad1!

Thus, all the white forces are in play. Unfortunately for Black, it's not possible to relocate his queen to a different safe square, due to its obligation to keep an eye on f7. Therefore, Black's reply is forced.

19...♗d6 20 ♗xh6!

Before penetrating via g6, White opens the g-file with this beautiful sacrifice.

20...gxh6 *(D)*

A final attempt to eliminate the bishop with 20...♘xb3 would be met with another devastating sacrifice: 21 ♗xg7! ♔xg7 22 ♘f5+.

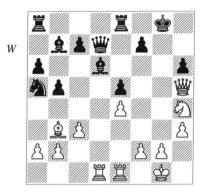

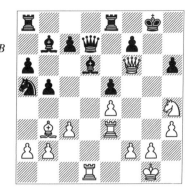

21 ♕g6+ ♔f8 22 ♕f6

The obvious threat is ♘g6+ followed by ♕h8#.

22...♔g8 23 ♖e3 *(D)*

1-0

The game is decided once the rook joins the battle. A slight but important inaccuracy in the opening (13...♕d7?!) left Black facing problems that that lasted right to the bitter end of the game.

An Inspiring Manoeuvre

Game 36

Rossolimo – Reissmann

San Juan 1967

Giuoco Piano

1 e4 e5 2 ♘f3 ♘c6 3 ♗c4 ♗c5

This is the *Giuoco Piano*, an opening we have already seen more than once in this book.

4 c3 ♘f6 5 d4 *(D)*

The basic ideas in this ancient opening have already been mentioned a few times. White aims to set up a solid centre with pawns on d4 and e4, so that he can claim a space advantage. Black will actively oppose this plan and stake his own claim in the centre.

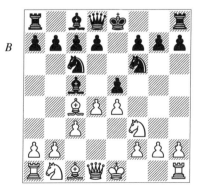

5...exd4 6 cxd4

Although this recapture is by far the most popular option, there is also an interesting alternative in 6 e5, which Black *must* meet with the thematic central counterblow 6...d5!. After 7 ♗b5 ♘e4 8 cxd4 ♗b6, White bases his further play on his slight space advantage (thanks to his advanced pawn on e5), while Black seeks pressure on d4.

6...♗b4+

Only by giving check can Black gain time to challenge White's central duo.

7 ♗d2

This is the main line in modern practice. An older and more aggressive line is the pawn sacrifice 7 ♘c3 (see Game 8) 7...♘xe4 8 0-0, which has been analysed extremely extensively and is considered at least OK for Black. But it's better to proceed without giving further details, as opening issues are not our main concern in this book.

7...♗xd2+ 8 ♘bxd2 *(D)*

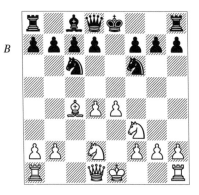

Don't you think that everything seems bright from White's perspective? All his minor pieces are developed, his king is ready to castle, and most importantly he has created his strong pawn-centre... Yet Black's strong reply will cause a major revision in this overview.

8...d5!

After this very well-timed advance, White's proud duo will not keep their posture. Suddenly, another typical structure, an isolated queen's pawn, emerges.

9 exd5 ♘xd5 10 ♕b3

Another reasonable option for White is 10 0-0 followed by ♘e5.

10...♘ce7

Black's obvious attempt to benefit from the uncastled king with 10...♕e7+? not only fails to bring a significant plus, but it even hands White a decisive advantage after 11 ♔f1!.

On the other hand, 10...♘a5 11 ♕a4+ (otherwise White must allow the undesirable exchange of his bishop) 11...♘c6 is a 'silent' draw offer, since if White plays 12 ♕b3, Black can repeat the position with 12...♘a5.

The decision in the game gives White some respite, but solidifies Black's blockade on d5. Such an approach is a fundamental strategy against an isolated queen's pawn.

11 0-0 c6

Consistently pursuing the plan of supporting d5.

12 ♖fe1 0-0

So far, both sides have played a reasonable game. White, as the possessor of an isolated pawn, needs to force the pace with dynamic moves and plans, so that he won't lose his temporary initiative in the middlegame.

13 a4 b6 *(D)*

This move unnecessarily transforms Black's b-pawn into a target. A playable alternative is 13...a5, to prevent the white a-pawn's march, while also seizing control over b4.

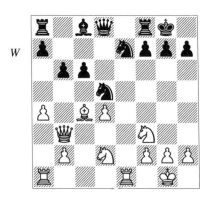

14 ♘e5!

White is playing dynamically. But what do we mean by 'dynamic'? It relates to plans based on the temporary or changing features of the position, rather than the static or more permanent ones. Generally we are talking about pawn-breaks and piece-play, especially when these pieces are able to gain time by creating threats or targeting weaknesses along the way. Black's c6-pawn has become a potentially vulnerable pawn after his last move, and Rossolimo duly acts according to this important nuance in the position.

14...♗b7

14...♗e6 would avoid some of the problems Black later experiences with this bishop.

15 a5 *(D)*

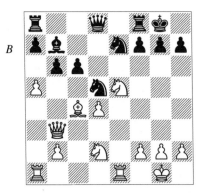

15...♖c8

Reissmann prepares a timely ...c5, and at the same time clears the a8-square for his bishop's retreat.

Black couldn't have reduced the pressure on the b-pawn with 15...b5 for concrete tactical reasons: 16 ♗xd5! ♕xd5 (16...♘xd5?! 17 a6! ♗c8 18 ♘xc6 ♕d6 19 ♕xd5! followed by ♘e7+) 17 a6 ♗c8 (White is better after 17...♕xb3 18 ♘xb3 ♗c8 19 ♘a5) 18 ♘xc6!.

16 ♘e4!

Forward! In isolated queen's pawn structures, the d-pawn provides solid control over c5 and e5, and it is very natural for the knights to use these squares as outposts. Here, however, the knight heads to g5 and thereafter aims to put pressure on the kingside.

16...♕c7?!

This thick-skinned move shows that Reissmann was still unaware of the dangers that were awaiting him. Both challenging the e5-knight with 16...f6, and preventing the other knight from jumping to g5 with 16...h6, are reasonable alternatives. Within a couple of dubious moves, we'll see that Black will face significant problems.

17 a6

A tough decision, since this advance closes the a-file. But Rossolimo has planned an abrupt transfer of the attack to the kingside, and therefore it makes sense to leave Black's bishop out of play forever.

17...♗a8 18 ♕h3

The third rank acts as a path for the major pieces to the kingside. It is quite likely that White will add to the pressure on f7 and h7 with ♘g5.

18...♘f4 19 ♕g4 ♘ed5 *(D)*

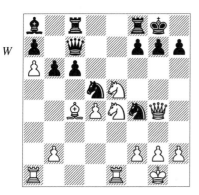

The black knights' activity is illusory, as White's kingside pieces are already generating significant attacking chances. There are many ways for White to increase the pressure. But with his next move, Rossolimo underlines the importance of using all possible reserves in the attack.

20 ♖a3!?

It is the rook's turn to use the third rank for its journey to the kingside. In the second game of the 2014 World Championship match (Carlsen-Anand – see Supplementary Game 4), a similar plan was the first step towards the young Norwegian's victory. Sometimes, ideas in these 'little' miniatures are inspiring, aren't they?

We should note that 20 ♘g5 is also very strong, one point being that 20...f6 allows 21 ♕xf4, due to the pin.

20...♘e6?

Now the rook will join the assault and the attack reaches its climax. Instead, trying to recall the out-of-play pieces to the game with 20...c5 might give some hope for the defence.

21 ♗xd5!

An important capture, as it forces the reply ...cxd5; after this exchange, Black's queenside pieces will be totally excluded from the defence.

21...cxd5 22 ♘f6+ ♔h8 23 ♕g6! *(D)*

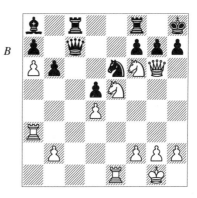

A marvellous move! The queen is untouchable, but it's also very hard for Black to tolerate her.

23...♕c2

Black has three possible pawn captures, but they all lead to disaster: 23...hxg6 24 ♖h3#, 23...fxg6 24 ♘xg6+ hxg6 25 ♖h3# or 23...gxf6 24 ♕xf6+ ♘g7 25 ♖g3 ♖g8 26 ♘xf7+.

With the move played, Black at least tries to defend h7 by using the *X-ray* theme. But this is a futile effort.

24 ♖h3! 1-0

The celebrated rook has the final word! It is obligatory to remove the queen, because of the threat of ♖xh7#, but this capture would result in the famous *Arabian Mate*: 24...♕xg6 25 ♘xg6+ fxg6 26 ♖xh7#. In the final position, almost all of White's forces have joined the attack on the kingside. Quite remarkable, isn't it?

When the Knight Takes the Stage...

Game 37
Spassky – Petrosian
World Ch match (19), Moscow 1969
Sicilian Defence

1 e4 c5 2 ♘f3 d6 3 d4 cxd4 4 ♘xd4 ♘f6 5 ♘c3 a6

This is the *Najdorf Variation*. One of the most important chess openings, it was a particular favourite of both Fischer and Kasparov, but has also been used by a great many other players.

6 ♗g5

This move provides a stiff test of Black's resources. Spassky aims to prevent Black's ...e5 push, which is one of the thematic ideas in the Najdorf (indeed, 5...a6 prepared it by preventing both ♗b5+ and ♘db5). Thus 6...e5?! is dubious as 7 ♗xf6 (7 ♘f5 is also possible) 7...♕xf6 8 ♘d5 ♕d8 9 ♘f5 gives White absolute control over the key d5-square.

6...♘bd7

We could have reached the ever-popular Poisoned Pawn Variation with 6...e6 7 f4 ♕b6 8 ♕d2 ♕xb2. In this 19th game of the World Championship match, Petrosian opts for a seemingly less risky line.

7 ♗c4 ♕a5 8 ♕d2 h6!?

Black tries to obtain the bishop-pair and delays the natural 8...e6 for now.

9 ♗xf6 ♘xf6 10 0-0-0

Thus White has completed his development. Petrosian must now secure his king's position, in order not to fall victim to a vigorous attack.

10...e6 11 ♖he1 ♗e7?! *(D)*

Given Black's failure to find a viable response to White's kingside attack in this game, many experts claimed that preparing ...0-0-0

with 11...♗d7 could have been a much better decision.

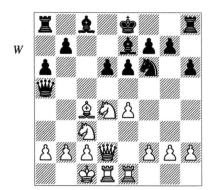

12 f4 0-0

Black has managed to evacuate his king from the centre, but opposite-side castling is always a razor-sharp scenario. One should bear in mind that White has a significant space advantage, and his kingside attack (led by a vanguard of pawns) can still harass Black's seemingly safe king.

13 ♗b3 ♖e8

Black prepares ...♗f8. While it was in keeping with Petrosian's style to secure his king before launching his own attack, in the context of a race to attack, this solid defensive plan can be considered too passive.

14 ♔b1

Sidestepping any potential dangers by leaving the possibly vulnerable c1-h6 diagonal, but there is more to say about this move, as it is *not* just a defensive move. Spassky prepares a tricky idea – ♘d5. For example, let's suppose it's White to move and he plays 15 ♘d5 on his next move. Black's obvious reply 15...♕xd2 will not come along with check, and therefore it will be possible for White to insert 16 ♘xf6+ and spoil Black's pawn-structure.

14...♗f8 *(D)*

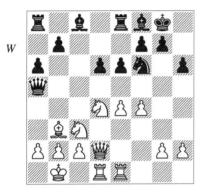

Now all the preparations are complete, and it's time for White to attack!

15 g4!

As mentioned in the notes to the previous move, 15 ♘d5!? might be an interesting alternative. Here, however, the purpose is to remove the defensive knight, rather than damaging Black's structure: 15...♕d8 (otherwise the kingside pawn-cover *would* be ruined) 16 ♘xf6+ ♕xf6 17 g4.

With his actual choice, Spassky opts instead to gain time by attacking the f6-knight. Note that White played this advance as a pawn sacrifice, rather than spending precious time preparing it. This is wholly in keeping with the requirements of the position. If Petrosian grabs the pawn, White aims to benefit from the open lines with his major pieces.

15...♘xg4

Although Black will be subjected to a vicious attack, he accepts the offer, as the g5 advance is dangerous in any case.

16 ♕g2 ♘f6

Trying to keep the g-file closed for some time with 16...e5 would weaken d5. It would also allow the b3-bishop to join the game immediately.

17 ♖g1 *(D)*

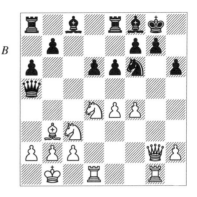

Thus the pressure on the g-file has been maximized. There are no forced lines after Spassky's sacrifice, indicating that his 'gift' has been grounded on positional evaluations, rather than pure calculation of variations. In any event, a challenging defensive duty awaits 'Iron Petrosian', who was famous for showing extraordinary defensive skills in the toughest positions one could imagine.

17...♗d7

A possible idea for White was harassing the knight with ♘f3 followed by e5. Black wants to hinder his opponent's plan: after 18 ♘f3 ♗c6 the e5 advance loses its effect.

18 f5 *(D)*

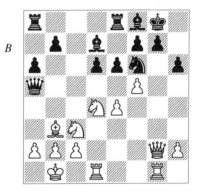

Regarding his opponent's thoughts, White stops Black's light-squared bishop from playing an active role on the long diagonal (...♗c6) by increasing the pressure on e6.

18...♔h8?!

This seems like a waste of time, but there is no ideal solution to Black's problems. Immobilizing White's pawns with 18...♕e5 seems like a reasonable option, but after 19 ♘f3 ♕c5

(19...♕f4 20 ♖d4 intending e5) 20 ♕h3 Black has little choice but to play 20...♔h8 in any case, when 21 ♘g5 retains good play.

19 ♖df1

White's major pieces are exerting enormous pressure on Black's kingside. Now, the concrete threat is fxe6 followed by ♖xf6!.

19...♕d8 *(D)*

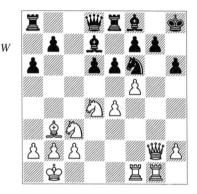

Supporting the f6-knight and thereby trying to prevent the exchange sacrifice. Throughout the game, Black's defensive duties have not allowed him to seek any active counterplay.

20 fxe6 fxe6 *(D)*

In order to overcome Black's defensive set-up, White needs to include his reserves in the attack. The queen, rooks and bishop are well-placed, and the knight on d4 is fine too. White should improve the other knight's position, right? But how?

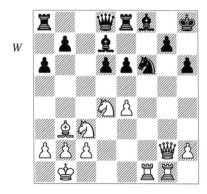

21 e5!!

Spassky benefits from the immobility of the f6-knight (if it moves, White will decisively strike with ♖xf8+ followed by ♕xg7#), and

clears the e4-square for his own knight's usage. Chess masters are distinguished from casual players by their good decisions at the most critical moments.

21...dxe5 22 ♘e4 *(D)*

After the knight's contribution, the ♖xf6! idea emerges as a new threat.

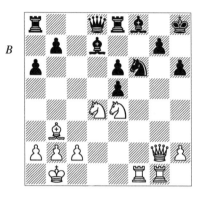

22...♘h5

Black has nothing better than to defend g7: 22...♘xe4? 23 ♖xf8+ and 24 ♕xg7#; 22...exd4 23 ♖xf6 (threatening ♖xh6+).

23 ♕g6

Pursuing the plan of harassing Black's knight.

23...exd4 *(D)*

23...♘f4 seems like the most reasonable option for Black, so how come Petrosian didn't go for it? While keeping the f-file closed for the moment would have forced Spassky to find a more creative solution, this was not an area in which he was exactly lacking. The exchange sacrifice with 24 ♖xf4 exf4 25 ♘f3 provides the deadly idea of locating one of the knights on g5 and winning on the spot.

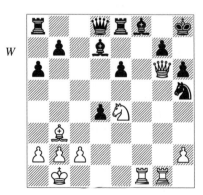

24 ♘g5!

Quite remarkable: just a few moves ago, the knight on c3 was a mere spectator. And now, it is precisely this piece that unlocks the door to victory.

1-0

Black resigns on seeing that after 24...hxg5 25 ♕xh5+ ♔g8 26 ♕f7+ ♔h7, the rook-lift to the h-file with 27 ♖f3 would be absolutely decisive.

Playing with Reversed Colours
Game 38
Dvoretsky – Damsky
Moscow 1970
King's Indian Attack

1 e4 e6

This is the *French Defence*, the main lines of which start after 2 d4 d5. But the current game transposes to a different opening within a few moves.

2 d3 d5 3 ♘d2

One might think that the knight's development via d2 is over-cautions. However, White doesn't want to allow his opponent to exchange queens at such an early stage with 3...dxe4 4 dxe4 ♕xd1+. Therefore, he aims to keep the d-file closed after a possible exchange on e4.

3...c5 4 ♘gf3 ♘c6 5 g3 *(D)*

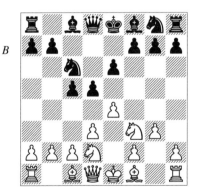

The *King's Indian Attack*. Would you think that playing a defence with reversed colours (and a tempo up) is a good approach? It is not easy to give a clear answer, as this is a lasting discussion within chess-players of all levels. Some claim that the extra tempo usually makes a large difference. Others think that by this method, White actually limits himself, as it is

hard to turn an essentially counterpunching set-up into an aggressive one, as long as the opponent adjusts his ambitions accordingly. Probably a recommendation such as 'play positions that you enjoy, without considering the influence of the colours' is closer to the right approach, while noting that it always depends on the specifics of each situation.

With the King's Indian Attack, White in general aims to keep the centre closed, and to generate a dangerous kingside attack.

5...♘f6 6 ♗g2 ♗e7 7 0-0 0-0 8 ♖e1 *(D)*

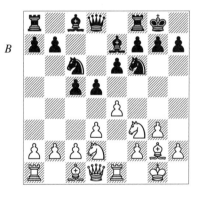

8...b6?!

Given that White intends to attack on the kingside, Black's natural counterplay should come on the queenside. Therefore expansion in this area of the board with 8...b5 can be considered a significant improvement over the text-move. Often when deciding between ...b6 and ...b5, Black must take into account an attempt by White to exploit the loosening effect of ...b5 by playing, e.g., a4, but this is unlikely to have much impact here, as there are few white pieces ready to take part in a queenside skirmish.

9 e5

An important advance, which, so to speak, divides the board in two: the pawn's presence on e5 keeps Black's queenside pieces at bay. On the other hand, eliminating White's e-pawn with ...f6 could prove to be a real concession, as this would expose weaknesses in Black's structure.

9...♘d7 10 ♘f1

Manoeuvring is a standard feature of closed positions. Compared to open positions, the game has a much slower pace, and therefore both sides can take their time to bring the pieces to their ideal positions.

In this case, White aims as far as possible to locate his pieces on the kingside, where he aims to break through.

10...♗b7 11 h4 (D)

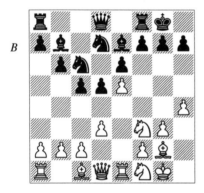

If it were an open position, then such an advance would be highly risky, as it exposes White's own king while also spending time on the wing that could better be spent in the centre. But with a closed centre, the pawn advance aims to support the kingside play, specifically on the dark squares.

11...♕c7

Black puts pressure on e5, even though White has no real difficulty defending this pawn. Black's idea is that giving some of White's pieces defensive obligations will make it harder for him to organize his attack. Nevertheless, the c7-square is not the most appropriate place for Black's queen, and we shall soon see why.

12 ♗f4!

The bishop reinforces the pawn and at the same time tries to benefit from its positioning on the same diagonal as Black's queen. This is not just an abstract notion, as it can support ideas like ♘e3xd5 or ♘1h2-g4-f6+, while hindering any ...f6 pawn-breaks.

12...b5

Black confesses that he squandered a tempo by playing the earlier 8...b6?!.

13 ♘1h2 (D)

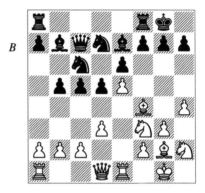

13...d4?!

One should think twice before advancing a pawn, as there is no going back. Also, don't forget that with each pawn advance, control over at least one square is weakened. Apparently, Damsky was seeking to prepare ...♘b6-d5. Tempting as it is to centralize the knight, with this pawn advance Black also loses control over e4, and this square will prove a useful transition point for White's forces. The penalty for this typical mistake will be harsh.

14 ♘g5!

White immediately targets h7 and at the same time opens up diagonals for both his queen and bishop.

14...h6 15 ♕h5!

After 14...h6, this pawn has become a natural target for White's upcoming sacrifices. Once White plays ♘e4, sacrificial ideas such as ♗xh6 and ♘g4xh6+ are highly worrying.

15...hxg5

Black can't eliminate White's e-pawn by 15...♘dxe5 because of 16 ♗xe5! ♘xe5 17 ♘xe6, with an advantage for White.

An attempt to ignore the sacrifice and generate queenside counterplay also ends badly for

Black: 15...♘b4 16 ♘g4 ♘xc2 (16...hxg5 17 hxg5, followed by ♘f6+, is similar to the game) 17 ♘xh6+ gxh6 18 ♕xh6 ♗xg5 (the only way to postpone checkmate on h7) 19 ♕xg5+ ♔h8 20 ♕h5+ (the bishop should stand in the front, so it can use the h6-square) 20...♔g8 21 ♗h6 and checkmate in a few moves.

In view of these concrete variations, Damsky decided to remove White's menacing knight.

16 hxg5 *(D)*

16... ♖fb8

The f8-square is cleared for either supporting the defence with ...♘f8, or as an escape-route for the king. Still, this preparatory move is insufficient to parry White's attacking plans.

17 ♘g4 ♘f8 18 ♘f6+! *(D)*

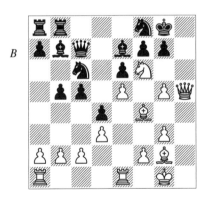

When on move 12 White located his dark-squared bishop on the same diagonal as Black's queen, we mentioned the possibility of this sacrifice. All the requirements are now present for this idea: White has accumulated many forces on the kingside, and Black handed over the e4-square.

We should underline another fact from the position: after the centre was closed by White's e5 advance, both sides have sought opportunities on opposite flanks. But when we look at the current position, we see that Black has not managed to make much progress on the queenside. Maybe his impotent play encouraged Dvoretsky to execute his aggressive plan.

18...♗xf6

18...gxf6 19 exf6 e5 (19...♗d6 20 ♕h6) 20 ♕h6 ♘e6 21 ♗e4 once again reminds us of the importance of the e4-square.

19 exf6 e5 *(D)*

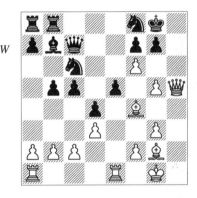

20 ♗d5!

The reserves keep joining the assault.

20...♖e8 *(D)*

The f4-bishop was taboo due to an *interference* theme: after 20...exf4 21 ♖e7!, the f7-square is very weak. There's not enough time to attack the other bishop either: 20...♖d8 21 ♔g2! ♘b4 22 ♖h1! (checkmate trumps everything) 22...♗xd5+ 23 f3 ♗xf3+ 24 ♔xf3 ♘g6 25 ♕h7+ ♔f8 26 ♕h8+! ♘xh8 27 ♖xh8# (Emms).

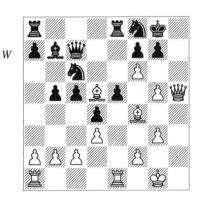

21 g6

White's pawns have advanced all the way to f6 and g6! Very elegant, isn't it?

21...♘d8 22 gxf7+ 1-0

Black resigned as after 22...♘xf7 23 ♕g5 g6 24 ♕h6 ♘e6 25 ♗xe6, mate on g7 is inevitable.

'Chinese Torture'

Game 39

Liu Wenzhe – Donner

Buenos Aires Olympiad 1978

Pirc Defence

1 e4 d6 2 d4 ♘f6 3 ♘c3 g6

The *Pirc Defence*. You can find another example of this system in Game 33.

4 ♗e2

This seemingly calm move is one of many valid options for White.

4...♗g7 5 g4!? *(D)*

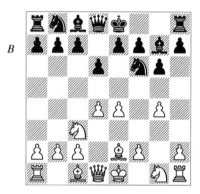

The flexible 4 ♗e2 was described as only 'seemingly' calm, since White can turn this move into the first step of an aggressive approach. Is it really logical to initiate a pawn-storm, even before Black has castled? Before criticizing, let's look at Liu Wenzhe's plan from a different angle: if Black, after weighing up the possible risks, decides to castle queenside, then how appropriate will White's moves look? The g4 advance may look a little misdirected, but it could form part of a space-grab, and is by no means any sort of fatal weakening. And in order to put his king on the queenside, Black will need to make some rather awkward and time-consuming moves; his set-up is very much geared towards kingside castling. Thus we can

view it as a trade-off with rather uncertain consequences, and the assessment will depend on the specifics of how both sides implement their plans. But if White plays many more moves that only make sense in the context of a king-side attack, he will be making a major commitment to a venture that may prove inappropriate.

On the other hand, a couple of moves later, Donner's decision to castle kingside will certainly render White's radical push logical.

5...h6

Black wants to maintains his knight's influence in the centre, and so prevents his opponent from harassing it with the g5 advance.

6 h3

It is not possible to develop the g1-knight without first protecting the pawn. With this modest move, White avoids burning his boats. The space-grabbing moves of the h- and g-pawns can also serve as a way to stifle Black's natural kingside play, and the time-loss is small since Black has spent a move on ...h6.

6...c5 *(D)*

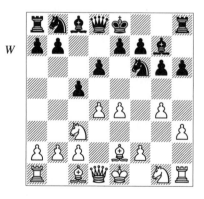

With this flanking blow, Black seeks to open the centre, which is a typical idea in such positions. From White's perspective, he has better chances of a successful attack on the wing if the centre is stable or closed.

7 d5 0-0 8 h4!?

6 h3 and just two moves later 8 h4... True, the first impression is quite odd, but White grounds his play on Black's king's placement and on the partly closed centre. A changed situation calls for a new plan.

8...e6

Insisting on a central break. But is there enough time to achieve this goal? We'll see...

9 g5!

When feasible, attack is the best form of defence. White reduces the pressure on his centre by forcing back the black knight.

9...hxg5 10 hxg5

The first mission is completed: the h-file is cleared for the rook's use.

10...♘e8 *(D)*

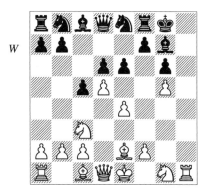

Liu Wenzhe's aggressive attitude in the opening has paid off: the open h-file now poses great danger to Black. When there's such a critical threat to the health of a king, other positional elements, such as development, pawn-structure, etc., may be of secondary importance.

In this case, White, who has laid many opening principles aside, needs to continue his plan with suitably dynamic moves. The Chinese master finds exactly the right way.

11 ♕d3!

Mission 2: her majesty should be transferred to the h-file as quickly as possible.

11...exd5

By opening the diagonal of his light-squared bishop and preventing ♕h3, Black aims to gain some time. As early as the 11th move, White's checkmate threats along the h-file have forced his opponent to race against time.

12 ♘xd5

It is very natural to establish a knight on an important central square. But can't White immediately bring his queen into the attack with 12 ♕g3 followed by 13 ♕h4? Here is a plausible line: 12...dxe4 13 ♕h4 f6 (half-heartedly opening the diagonal, but what else can Black do?) 14 ♗c4+ ♖f7 15 ♕h7+ ♔f8 16 ♕xg6 and White's attack remains dangerous.

12...♘c6?!

Black cannot tolerate even a tiny loss of time in this razor-sharp position. Donner had to take precautions against White's wicked thoughts along the open h-file. A better option is 12...♘c7, challenging the strong knight on d5, while at the same time vacating e8 for the rook's use.

13 ♕g3!

No time to lose – White is heading for mate!

13...♗e6 14 ♕h4 f5 *(D)*

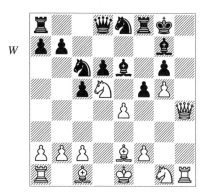

This is Donner's plan: f7 is vacated as an escape-route for Black's king. This seems perfectly safe and logical, but does White have any dramatic ideas to continue his attack? Now it's time for calculation, so let's think...

15 ♕h7+ ♔f7 16 ♕xg6+!!

A key sacrifice to overcome Black's defensive set-up.

16...♔xg6

After 16...♔g8, the game will end even more quickly: 17 ♕h7+ ♔f7 18 ♗h5#.

17 ♗h5+ ♔h7 18 ♗f7+ ♔h6 *(D)*

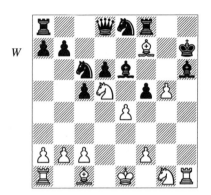

19 g6+!

Foreseeing this move was the most difficult part of the combination. White aims to capture on h6 with the c1-bishop, which has been sleeping up to now.

19...♔g7 20 ♗xh6+ 1-0

Donner resigned, as it is mate after 20...♔h8 21 ♗xf8+ ♕h4 22 ♖xh4#.

It is quite remarkable that Liu Wenzhe's attack succeeded so easily. After all, he hasn't castled, and hasn't even touched his pieces on a1, g1 and h1. What is the explanation? Well, mating attacks outweigh every other positional consideration and become decisive factors, as long as the essential preconditions are met.

Firepower in the Critical Zone

Game 40

Kasparov – Marjanović

Malta Olympiad 1980

Queen's Indian Defence

1 d4 ♘f6 2 c4 e6 3 ♘f3 b6

The *Queen's Indian Defence*. Games 16 and 24 are two other examples of this defence you can find in our book.

4 g3

White wants to oppose the b7-bishop on the long diagonal. This is the main line, but of course there are several other reasonable options for White at this point.

4...♗b7 5 ♗g2 ♗e7 6 0-0 *(D)*

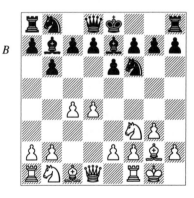

6...0-0

Up to this point, both sides have developed their positions in a rather natural manner. But Kasparov now radically sharpens the character of the game with an ambitious move:

7 d5!?

Doesn't this just blunder a pawn? Not exactly; with this enterprising pawn sacrifice, White aims to shut Black's b7-bishop out of play, at least for a time, and to create a strong outpost for the knight after the ♘h4-f5 manoeuvre.

7...exd5 8 ♘h4

It is really important to clear the diagonal of the g2-bishop while initiating the knight's manoeuvre: this way, the cxd5 idea has become a concrete threat. If Black wants to maintain his material advantage, then he has to protect the pawn before continuing his development.

8...c6 9 cxd5 ♘xd5 10 ♘f5

This position is the real consequence of the pawn sacrifice. Now, White's knight on f5 is a menacing force, since knights are highly effective when they are close to their targets. The first high-level game with this pawn sacrifice –

Polugaevsky-Korchnoi, Candidates match (12), Buenos Aires 1980 (Supplementary Game 3) – shows the attacking potential of the knight: 10...♗c5 11 e4 ♘e7?! 12 ♘xg7! ♔xg7 13 b4 with an advantageous position for White.

10...♘c7 (D)

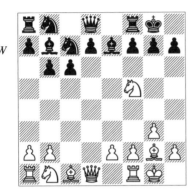

In his turn, Black wants to relieve his position with a timely ...d5 advance.

11 ♘c3 d5 12 e4 ♗f6

The exchange of queens is not possible yet: 12...dxe4 13 ♘xe4 ♕xd1?? 14 ♘xe7+! (an important *zwischenzug*) 14...♔h8 15 ♖xd1 and White is a piece up.

13 exd5

With this exchange, Kasparov wants the d5-pawn to close the diagonal for a while, so that it will be quite hard for Black's pieces on the queenside to participate in the battle.

13...cxd5 14 ♗f4 ♘ba6 15 ♖e1 (D)

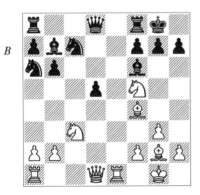

15...♕d7

Black has more or less completed his development, and now it is time to exhibit a constructive plan. While this move isn't actually an error,

the faulty follow-up suggests that Marjanović was already drifting at this point. A well-known strategic method to neutralize pressure is to give back the material advantage. In this sense, even if it causes Black to lose his d5-pawn, the offside knight could rejoin the fight with 15...♘c5.

16 ♗h3

The bishop finds a way to be effective once again on another diagonal. Suddenly 17 ♘h6+ followed by 18 ♗xd7 is a dangerous threat.

16...♔h8? (D)

Surprisingly, Black's best move is 16...♕d8, when it is very hard to find a path to any meaningful advantage for White.

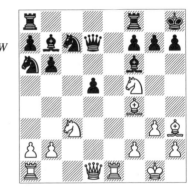

After the black king's sidestep into the corner, the threat disappears along with the ♘h6+ idea. But the black queen's loose position still gives White an opportunity to transfer his pieces to the kingside, where the real battle will occur.

17 ♘e4!

Kasparov is not worried about losing more material on the queenside. He thinks (and knows!) so, because the most important factor is the amount of firepower in the critical zone.

17...♗xb2 18 ♘g5!

As mentioned before, knights are more effective when they are closer to their targets. Also, discovered-attack ideas reappear now that the h3-bishop is protected.

18...♕c6 19 ♘e7 ♕f6 (D)

It is quite understandable for the black queen to insist on staying on its third rank. Otherwise, Black would be helpless against ♕h5 followed by ♗e5; e.g., 19...♕c3 20 ♕h5 h6 21 ♗e5.

After Black's move, the same idea would fail for the moment: 20 ♕h5 h6 21 ♗e5? ♕xg5.

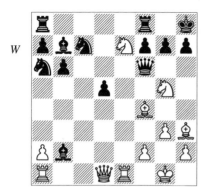

Still, there is another way to transform the pressure on the h-file into a concrete advantage. Of course, Kasparov does not miss this opportunity.

20 ♘xh7!

The knight cannot be taken: White wins after 20...♔xh7 21 ♕h5+.

20...♕d4 21 ♕h5

One by one, White accumulates his forces on the kingside. It is simply impossible to hold on against this unbearable attack.

21...g6 22 ♕h4 ♗xa1 23 ♘f6+ *(D)*

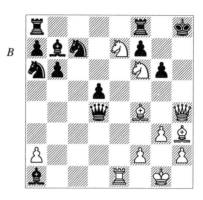

1-0

Looking at the final position, it is remarkable that all the white pieces, excluding the lonely a2-pawn, are positioned on the kingside.

This emphasizes that it is much more important to have more firepower in the critical zone, than a material advantage in less important areas of the board.

Playing *à la* Petrosian

Game 41
Kasparov – Petrosian
Bugojno 1982
Bogo-Indian Defence

1 d4 ♘f6 2 c4 e6 3 ♘f3 ♗b4+ *(D)*

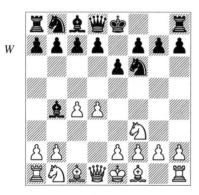

The *Bogo-Indian Defence*. In this system, Black often locates his central pawns on dark squares to answer his opponent's advances in this area of the board. This fits in well with the idea of exchanging off the dark-squared bishop so it is not left standing passively behind the c7-d6-e5 pawn-chain.

However, this is not the only plan for Black, and in this game we see Petrosian opting for a set-up with ...d5, which is somewhat similar to *Catalan* structures. The danger is that the c8-bishop may prove hard to develop.

4 ♗d2 ♕e7

Quite consistent with the previously mentioned plan. Her majesty protects the threatened bishop, while at the same time preparing a possible ...d6 and ...e5.

5 g3 ♗xd2+

Black could have postponed this exchange of bishops, and continued to press the centre with 5...♘c6.

6 ♕xd2!?

Isn't capturing with the knight more natural? It might seem so, but Kasparov wants to place his knight on c3, where it has the most influence over the central squares, and judges that this is more important than simply developing as quickly as possible.

6...0-0 7 ♗g2 d5

A radical change in the game plan: now Black's pawns in the centre are placed on light squares. This approach makes it more difficult for Black's light-squared bishop to join the game. Still, we should mention that White's slight plus can easily evaporate if he makes a few imprecise moves.

8 0-0 *(D)*

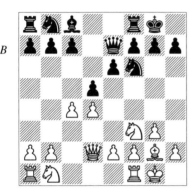

Even though the game started with a different defence, this looks like a typical position for the *Catalan Opening* (1 d4 d5 2 c4 e6 3 ♘f3 ♘f6 4 g3 is one of the main versions of this opening, but there are some variant forms and many possible move-orders).

Now, Black has to solve the perennial problem of developing the light-squared bishop. But just at the most inappropriate moment, Petrosian carelessly releases the tension between the central pawns, and this leads to a worse position for him.

8...dxc4?

After this capture, White acquires a central pawn-majority. Kasparov's reply will show an additional benefit of him not rushing to bring out his queen's knight.

9 ♘a3!

When knights have logical paths to the centre or effective posts, there is nothing wrong with them initiating their journey from the rim. In this case, the knight's a3-c4 route aims to prevent Black's desired ...e5 advance, and thereby underline the passivity of the c8-bishop.

9...c5 10 dxc5 ♕xc5 11 ♖ac1 ♘c6 12 ♘xc4 *(D)*

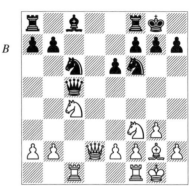

Thus, White has regained his pawn with an advantageous position.

12...♕e7 13 ♘fe5 ♘xe5 14 ♘xe5 ♘d5 15 ♖fd1!

Although exchanging pieces in cramped positions might be a relief in most cases, here it is quite difficult for Black to find a constructive plan. On the other hand, Kasparov has a very simple and comfortable game. With the text-move, he seizes control over two open files. There's no need to be in a hurry here, since Black is bound hand and foot.

15...♘b6 16 ♕a5!

White prevents an exchange of rooks with this powerful move. To give an exemplary variation, 16...♖d8? 17 ♘c4! ♖xd1+ 18 ♖xd1 leaves Black almost paralysed.

16...g6 17 ♖d3 ♘d5

Black cannot find any logical follow-up, while Kasparov improves his position step by step. Apparently Black was planning a possible queen exchange after ...♕b4. Even if this idea occurs on the board, White would still have the upper hand, but why should White give some hope to his opponent unnecessarily?

18 e4! *(D)*

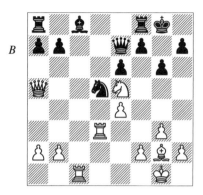

B

18...♘b6

Unfortunately, this passive retreat was forced. 18...♕b4 fails to 19 ♖xd5!, while 18...♘f6 would be met by 19 ♖c7, when it's very difficult for Black to hold the position.

19 ♗f1

Kasparov wants to use all his resources. The long diagonal was closed when White played e4. Therefore, the bishop heads to a different diagonal, which will be available after the rook vacates d3.

19...♖e8 20 ♖dd1 ♖f8

It's hard to find even a single move for Black!

21 a3 ♔g7 22 b3 ♔g8 23 a4

Slowly but surely, the decisive strike is prepared.

23...♖d8 *(D)*

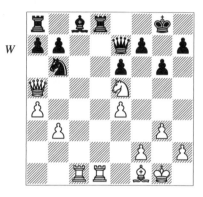

W

24 ♕c5! 1-0

Black cannot avoid material loss: 24...♕xc5 25 ♖xd8+ ♕f8 26 ♖xf8+ ♔xf8 27 ♖c7 and it's impossible to resist against the ideas of ♖xf7+ and a5.

An 11-Year-Old Girl

Game 42

Costa – J. Polgar

Biel 1987

English Opening

1 d4 ♘f6 2 c4 c5

An invitation to either the *Modern Benoni* (3 d5 e6) or the *Benko Gambit* (3 d5 b5); Judit would no doubt have chosen the latter, as it was one of her favourite openings in her early years. However, aiming to reach a calmer position, White declines such challenges.

3 ♘f3

This position is generally classified as an English Opening (1 c4) because it can arise via 1 c4 c5 2 ♘f3 ♘f6 3 d4. However, this specific position tends to come about most often from the Benoni move-order seen in our game; opening naming can seem a little arbitrary at times.

3...cxd4 4 ♘xd4 e5

With her enterprising approach, Black does not worry about her backward d-pawn, and questions the d4-knight's powerful stance in the centre.

5 ♘b5

This move is intended to prevent Black's ...d5 advance, and to go on to exploit the weak d5-square in a slow positional struggle. It's true that after 5...d5 6 cxd5 ♘xd5? 7 ♕xd5! ♕xd5 8 ♘c7+ White wins a piece. But Judit Polgar, who was later to become the strongest female chess-player of all time, shows another path for Black:

5...d5!? *(D)*

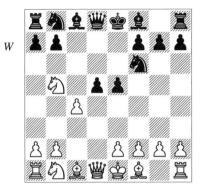

No matter what! Of course, Black was aware that it wasn't possible to recapture on d5. But she voluntarily gets rid of the trouble spot, instead of trying to solve its problems throughout the game.

6 cxd5 ♗c5 *(D)*

This is the *Vaganian Gambit*. Black intends to develop her pieces very actively, and just leave the pawn on d5. Black is claiming that the d5-pawn will only get in the way of White's pieces, and serve almost like an 'umbrella' for Black's own pieces, protecting them from frontal attack and making it hard for White to initiate exchanges. Of course, this is a genuine gambit, so eventually Black will need either to generate a substantial initiative or to win back the pawn.

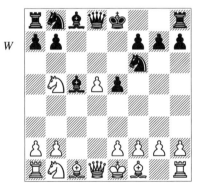

7 ♘5c3

Costa retreats his knight, as sooner or later, Black's ...a6 and ...b5 advance would come along with tempo. Still, it's rarely OK to make several moves with one piece while there are undeveloped forces in our camp. This is an encouraging sign for the gambiteer.

7...0-0 8 g3

Allowing the bishop to set its eyes on f2 seems very risky, although this move is one of the most popular options.

8...♘g4!?

Consequently, Black initiates an attack on f2 while clearing the way for the ...f5 advance.

9 e3 f5 10 ♗g2?!

When making each move, even if it is a normal developing move within a plan, it's important to take our opponent's ideas into account. Once we pause to make this assessment, it is clear that Black is aiming to open lines with ...f4, and we can see that White's simple developing move may be an error. To avoid falling victim to Black's all-out attack, White should have opted for 10 ♗e2, which prevents the advance of the f-pawn for the moment.

10...f4 11 h3?! *(D)*

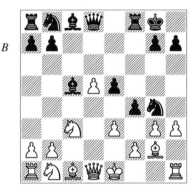

But this is too much.

11...♘xf2!

White's king is dangerously exposed.

12 ♔xf2 fxe3++ 13 ♔e1 ♖f2

After a serious of forced moves, another critical moment has been reached.

14 ♖g1?

It is not easy to make the psychological adjustment, as White early in the game, to defending against a vicious attack. Maybe this is the reason why White instinctively defended the bishop. In her own analysis of the game, Polgar mentions that 14 d6 (in connection with the ♕d5+ idea) is a more resilient way to handle the position.

14...♕f8 15 ♕d3 *(D)*

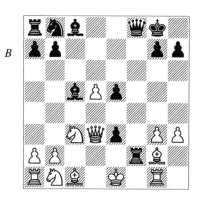

15...♘a6!

For the attack to be successful, all available forces must be brought into play. While indirectly defending e3 (16 ♗xe3? ♘b4! 17 ♕e4 ♘c2+), Black aims to include her knight in the attack.

16 a3

Fending off the threats must take priority over everything else.

16...♗f5! 17 ♗e4

White tries to keep the position closed as long as possible. But this is not a realistic expectation, since Black's forces will keep coming and coming.

17...♗xe4 18 ♕xe4

Polgar took her time analysing the seemingly more natural 18 ♘xe4, which is met by 18...e2! (threatening ...♖f1+) 19 ♘bd2 ♖h2 20

♘f3 ♗xg1 21 ♘xh2 ♘c5! (with perfect timing, the knight joins the game) 22 ♕xe2 ♗xh2 23 ♕xh2 ♘xe4 and, with a significant lead in development, Black will easily convert her advantage into victory.

18...♗d4

The c5-square is cleared for the knight's use.

19 ♗xe3 ♘c5! *(D)*

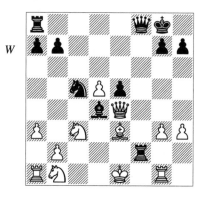

20 ♗xd4 exd4!?

Of course, snatching the queen was possible. But apparently, continuing with the attack was more attractive for the Hungarian.

21 ♕xd4 ♖e8+

With the rook's participation, Black emphasizes that she was using all available forces, from A to Z!

22 ♔d1 ♕f3+ 0-1

It is checkmate after 23 ♘e2 ♕xe2+ 24 ♔c1 ♘b3#.

Opening a Dangerous File
Game 43
W. Watson – Meduna
Prague 1992
Caro-Kann Defence

1 e4 c6 2 d4 d5 3 ♘d2 dxe4 4 ♘xe4 ♘d7

This is the *Modern Variation* of the *Caro-Kann Defence* (1 e4 c6). Several former World Champions, most notably Smyslov and Karpov, were adherents of this solid system. Black does not want his bishop to get kicked around after 4...♗f5, nor does he like the doubled pawns

arising after 4...♘f6 5 ♘xf6+, so he opts for preparing ...♘gf6 instead.

5 ♘g5!? *(D)*

White refrains from a possible knight exchange on f6 (or e4). The knight voluntarily leaves its central post, but on the other hand it is getting closer to its probable targets.

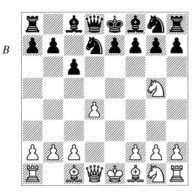

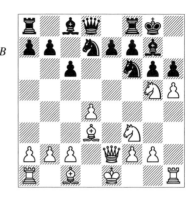

5...Ngf6

Here, 5...h6?! 6 Ne6! would be a nasty surprise. In that case, since the knight is taboo (6...fxe6?? 7 Wh5+, mating), Black would have to be content with losing his bishop-pair after 6...Wb6 7 Nxf8.

6 Bd3 g6

In modern opening practice, Black normally prepares to develop the bishop via 6...e6. The problems that Black faced in the current game were part of the reason for that.

7 N1f3 Bg7 8 We2 *(D)*

Watson cleverly delays castling with a useful waiting move.

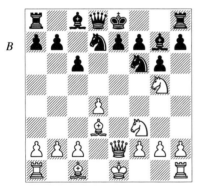

8...0-0 9 h4!

That was the idea! White can attack Black's pawn-chain with h5 whenever the conditions are right. Thereby the h-file will be cleared and Black's king will be the subject of a dangerous attack. Actually this was the main problem of 6...g6.

9...h6 10 h5! *(D)*

Chaos on the board! Unfortunately for Black, the mayhem occurs just around his king.

10...Nxh5?!

Was it possible to accept the knight sacrifice? It's very concrete and complex, so let's analyse: 10...hxg5 11 h6 Bh8 12 Nxg5! (threatening Bxg6, followed by h7+/Ne6+) 12...Nb6 13 h7+ Kg7 and after, e.g., 14 Wd2!? Black's vulnerability on h6 puts him in a difficult situation.

11 g4?! *(D)*

11 Nxf7! Rxf7 (11...Kxf7 12 We4) 12 Bxg6 exploits Black's weak light squares.

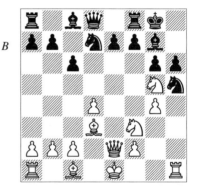

11...Nhf6?

This natural retreat is unfortunately faulty. However, 11...Ng3!? is very interesting: 12 fxg3 hxg5 (what an odd pawn-structure!) and after the removal of the menacing g5-knight, Black's defensive idea with ...Nf6 would grant him a playable position.

After the move played, Watson is able to land a strong sacrificial blow similar to one we mentioned at the start of the game.

12 Ne6!

White's play on the light squares and the rook's power on the h-file make his attack nearly irresistible.

12...fxe6

Inserting the check 12...♕a5+ fails to help: 13 ♗d2 ♕b6 14 ♘xg7 and this time the game comes to an end from the attack on h6.

13 ♕xe6+ ♖f7

13...♔h7 was not possible: 14 ♗xh6! ♗xh6 15 g5 ♘b6 16 ♖xh6+ ♔g7 17 ♖xg6+ ♔h8 18 ♖h6+ ♔g7 19 ♖h7+! (a neat way to open up the 6th rank) 19...♘xh7 20 ♕g6+ ♔h8 21 ♕xh7#. When the line progresses with forced moves, it is not that difficult to calculate, right?

14 ♗xg6 ♕f8 15 g5

This is how the initiative works: successive strikes give the defender no time to construct a defence, as all he can do is parry threats.

15...♘d5 16 gxh6 ♘e5 *(D)*

Meduna was counting on this defensive resource. But the game abruptly ends, as White's attack on the h-file rises on the occasion.

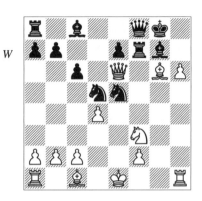

17 ♗h7+! 1-0

Black resigned after this classy *decoy* sacrifice: 17...♔xh7 18 hxg7+ ♔xg7 19 ♕h6+ ♔g8 20 ♕h8# or 17...♔h8 (a more resilient try) 18 hxg7+ ♕xg7 19 ♗e4+! (protecting the knight is important) 19...♔g8 20 ♕xe5 with a decisive material advantage for White (Stohl).

A Sacrifice to be Proud of

Game 44
Handke – Murdzia
Hamburg 2002
Sicilian Defence

1 e4 c5 2 ♘f3 d6 3 d4 cxd4 4 ♘xd4 ♘f6 5 ♘c3 a6 *(D)*

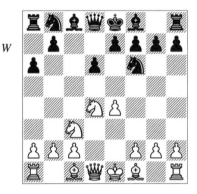

This is the *Sicilian Najdorf*. In this complex variation, Black's little pawn move has two main aims. Firstly, it prepares ...b5, when the ...b4 idea harasses White's knight on c3, which affects the battle for the central squares. Generally Black should not rush to fling his b-pawn down the board, but the idea is present in the background at least. Also, the move ...a6 covers the b5-square. This rules out ♘db5 so that Black can play ...e6 or especially ...e5 without d6 coming under immediate attack.

To understand the subtleties and nuances (such as move-orders, etc.) in this high-level defensive set-up, one needs to have not only theoretical knowledge, but also experience.

6 ♖g1!?

This weird move declares White's intention of launching a pawn-storm. Similar to Black's ...b5, here White wants to harass the f6-knight with the g4-g5 advance, and thereby seize control over the key central square d5.

6...♘c6

This is one of many valid options, which include 6...e5 and 6...b5. Apparently, Murdzia was planning to meet the flank attack with central play, which is a highly thematic approach.

7 g4 ♘xd4 8 ♕xd4 e5 *(D)*

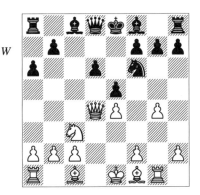

As grabbing the g4-pawn would involve significant risks, Black tries to equalize by attacking the centralized queen.

9 ♕a4+

Despite the apparent loss of time, there is a logical explanation for this type of check. White is seeking to disharmonize Black's forces on the queenside, and for this purpose he is content to lose a tempo and make another move with his queen.

9...♗d7

9...♕d7? 10 ♗b5! would be a swift loss.

10 ♕b3

While Black has gained the move ...♗d7 almost for free, it isn't a clear gain, since the bishop is ineffective on this square, and may need to move again.

10...b5 11 g5 ♗e6 *(D)*

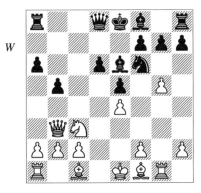

It looks like White's fancy footwork has only succeeded in landing his queen in a most

unfortunate situation. Now, 12 ♕a3 and 12 ♕b4 will both be met by a discovered attack with 12...d5, winning material. The only other obvious try, 12 ♘d5, fails to 12...♘xe4, when White has very little compensation for the loss of his e-pawn.

But sometimes in chess, the right solutions lie behind the moves and plans that we refuse even to consider at first glance.

12 gxf6!!

Wouldn't Nezhmetdinov be proud of this sacrifice? (see Nezhmetdinov-Chernikov, Rostov-on-Don 1962 – Supplementary Game 2).

12...♗xb3 13 axb3

Now White's intentions are clear: while d5 will be a strong outpost for the knight, the removal of the pawn on f6 (which causes significant discomfort in Black's camp) will open lines, which suits White's bishop-pair. But on the other hand, Black can hardly tolerate leaving this pawn on f6.

13...♕xf6?

This loses. After 13...gxf6 14 ♘d5, White obtains marvellous compensation, but the game is very far from clear.

14 ♗g5 ♕g6 *(D)*

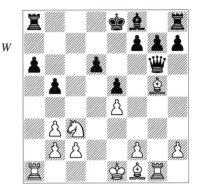

At first glance, 15 ♗xb5+ axb5 16 ♖xa8+ ♔d7 looks good for White, since he regains some of his lost material. But Black still has some threats under his belt: one idea is ...f6, exploiting the pin along the g-file, while ...b4 would make e4 vulnerable. Therefore in this variation, White must settle for a repetition with 17 ♖a7+ and ♖a8+, etc. (While Black can avoid an immediate draw, he cannot do so advantageously.)

There is a well-known chess saying: "When you spot a good move, look for a better one!". A great example is awaiting us.

15 Ξxa6!!

This is a much better (and spectacular!) way to benefit from the a4-e8 diagonal's vulnerability. The rook is untouchable on account of the checkmate (15...Ξxa6 16 ♗xb5+ Ξc6 17 ♗xc6#), and ♗xb5# is now a concrete threat, because its protection has been removed. In desperation, Black tries to stop these deadly ideas.

15...Ξb8 16 Ξa8!!

That's creativity! When Handke renews his threat of ♗xb5#, Black has nothing to do but to close the diagonal.

16...f6 17 Ξxb8+ ♔d7 18 ♗xb5+ *(D)*

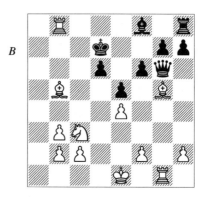

B

Now White is material up, but in any case there is no salvation against his all-out attack.

18...♔c7 19 ♗e8! 1-0

Black has managed to prevent the checkmate, but not the loss of his queen.

Another Fabulous Blocking Idea

Game 45

J. Polgar – Berkes

Budapest 2003

French Defence

1 e4 e6

The *French Defence*. This opening can lead to a wide variety of different structures, and frequently results in quite messy positions. In principle, however, Black aims to counter his opponent's centre by locating his own central pawns on light squares. In that respect, it is a solid approach. The obvious drawback, which it shares with the Queen's Gambit Declined, is that it leaves the light-squared bishop behind the pawn-chain.

2 d4 d5 3 ♘c3 ♘f6 4 ♗g5 dxe4

Releasing the tension means surrendering the centre. This can often leave Black with a solid but somewhat passive position.

5 ♘xe4 ♗e7 6 ♗xf6

In order to maintain the knight's effective position on e4, Polgar is content to give up her bishop.

6...♗xf6 7 ♘f3 0-0 8 ♕d2

Although a plan with kingside castling is completely playable, Black's plan against this timid idea with ...♘d7 and ...c5 (or ...e5) might lead to a very dull, and near-to-equal position. The position would be more or less equal once Black's light-squared bishop finds its way to freedom.

8...♘d7 9 0-0-0 *(D)*

Opposite-side castling suddenly creates a sharp position. With his next move, Berkes preserves his bishop-pair and aims to support his desired ...c5 advance.

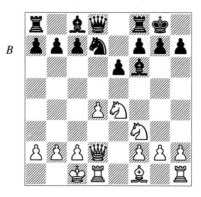

B

9...♗e7 10 ♗d3 b6

Now that Black needs just one more move to solve his bishop's perennial problem, White must launch her planned kingside attack very quickly. h7 is the most natural target, and can be attacked right away by two of White's minor pieces.

11 ♘eg5! h6

11...g6? is another way to cover h7, but the simple advance 12 h4, followed by h5, would force open the h-file. The safest option for Black is 11...♗xg5 12 ♘xg5 ♘f6, which, although unambitious since Black has given up his main trump, i.e. the bishop-pair, leaves him at just a slight disadvantage.

But what about the text-move?

12 ♗h7+

This typical check pushes the king to the corner. As White's main attacking front is the h-file, luring the king to it with gain of tempo is very logical.

12...♔h8 13 ♗e4

The bishop has completed its mission, and doesn't want to obstruct the h-file any more. This retreat comes with tempo, demonstrating a drawback of ...b6.

13...hxg5? *(D)*

13...♗xg5 is again a safer option.

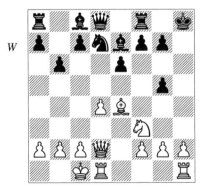

But now we might wonder if Polgar was wrong after all. It seems like 14 ♗xa8? g4 followed by ...♗g5 is winning for Black!

14 g4!!

Capturing the rook isn't obligatory. After this outstanding blockading idea, it will be impossible to stop the attack on the h-file. After 14 h4?, Black's reply 14...g4 would keep White's

front closed, and the text-move aims to prevent this. As the last few moves were more or less forced, it appears that Polgar had seen this strong idea even before playing 11 ♘eg5!.

14...♖b8 15 h4 *(D)*

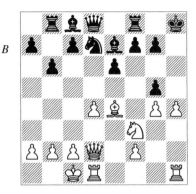

15...g6

As it is not possible to keep the h-file closed after 15...gxh4 16 g5!, Black seeks salvation by closing the bishop's diagonal, and at the same time by providing a safe square (g7) for his king.

16 hxg5+ ♔g7 17 ♕f4! *(D)*

Accuracy right to the end: it is very important to transfer the queen to the h-file as quickly as possible.

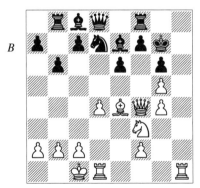

17...♗b7

The attempt to counter White's plan with 17...♖h8 fails because it leaves the f7-pawn less well protected: 18 ♖xh8 ♕xh8 (18...♔xh8 19 ♕xf7 followed by ♖h1+ is decisive) 19 ♘e5! ♘xe5 20 ♕xe5+ ♔g8 21 ♕xc7 and White wins.

18 ♖h7+!! *(D)*

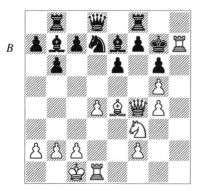

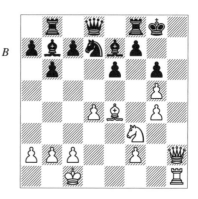

The quickest and most effective way to bring the queen to the h-file.

18...♗xh7 19 ♕h2+ ♔g8 20 ♖h1 *(D)*

As it's not possible to endure White's attack on the h-file any longer, Black desperately looks for ways to prolong the struggle.

20...♗xg5+ 21 ♘xg5 ♕xg5+ 22 f4 ♕xf4+ 23 ♕xf4 ♗xe4 24 ♕xe4 1-0

Effective usage of the h-file was the key element in White's majestic victory. What was the hero behind the curtains? Of course the fantastic blockading idea!

In an earlier game, a surprisingly similar motif occurred:

A Similar Case:

Forintos – Zedek
Imperia 1991
Position after 16...♕e7-d8

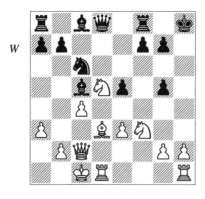

In similar fashion to the J.Polgar-Berkes game that we've just analysed, the h-file is once again the decisive element in this battle. Forintos finds a sacrificial way to attack Black's king, which has been more or less abandoned to its fate by the defensive forces:

17 g4!!

17 h4 is less effective due to 17...g4, so White sacrifices his g-pawn to block the g4-square.

17...♗xg4 18 h4! f5 *(D)*

It would be checkmate after 18...♗xf3 19 hxg5+ ♗xh1 20 ♕h2+ ♔g8 21 ♕h7#.

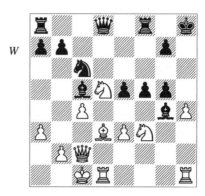

19 hxg5+ ♔g8 20 g6

Not allowing the king to escape.

20...♗xe3+ 21 ♘xe3 ♖f6 1-0

This inspiring game was analysed as an exercise in *Attack and Defence* (Batsford 1998), one of the works of the famous chess trainer Mark Dvoretsky and his star pupil Artur Yusupov.

The Aura of Magnus Carlsen

Game 46

Hammer – Carlsen

World Under-14 Ch, Kallithea 2003

Pirc Defence

1 ♘f3 d6 2 d4 ♘f6 3 ♘bd2 g6 4 e4

Here a form of the *Pirc Defence* has been reached via a different move-order. Systems such as the Pirc, Modern and King's Indian allow Black to form his defensive set-up almost regardless of what White is doing.

4...♗g7 5 ♗d3 0-0 6 0-0 *(D)*

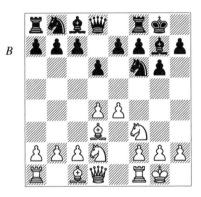

Both sides have castled, and now it's time for them to generate a short-term plan. For the moment, Black's fianchettoed bishop sets its eyes on d4. In order to support his bishop, Carlsen increases his pressure against this key square, and forces his opponent to make a decision about the central structure.

6...♘c6

A provocative move: in the event of 7 d5 ♘b8, White has gained time but slightly compromised his strong central stance. Black could then attack the d5-pawn with ...c6. Therefore, Hammer doesn't want to take a committal decision, and simply strengthens his d4-pawn instead.

7 c3 e5 8 h3 *(D)*

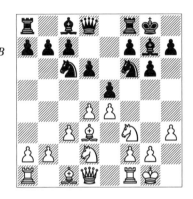

White restrains Black's bishop (...♗g4), so that it won't be able to step up the pressure on d4 by pinning the f3-knight.

8...♘h5!?

But Black is stubborn in his assault on d4: now he opens up the diagonal of the other bishop. ...♘h5-f4 is a typical knight manoeuvre in positions like this, and is encouraged by the fact that White has played h3, as kicking the knight away from f4 with g3 is nearly impossible since it would leave the h3-pawn hanging.

Hammer cannot tolerate the pressure any more, and decides to release the tension with his next move.

9 dxe5 ♘f4

In reply, Black inserts a neat *zwischenzug* (in-between move), and suddenly sharpens the seemingly-calm position.

10 ♗b5 ♘xe5 11 ♘xe5 ♕g5! *(D)*

Threatening both checkmate and ...♘xh3+. Although it wouldn't be fair to call this position worse for White, it is not a very comfortable situation to handle.

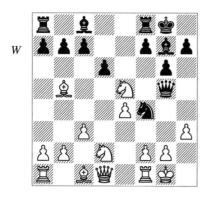

W

12 ♘g4 ♕xb5

After regaining the material, Black's idea is to acquire the bishop-pair with ...♘e2+ followed by ...♘xc1.

13 ♘b3 ♘e2+ 14 ♔h1 ♗xg4

A little change in the plan: suddenly Carlsen thinks that opening up the h-file, and creating some problems in White's structure, is more important. Of course, capturing with 14...♘xc1 was possible as well.

15 hxg4 ♖ae8 16 ♗e3?

The penalty for this miscalculation will be harsh. White has besieged the black knight within his own camp and now he aims to trap it with ♖e1. Quite dangerous, right? Not exactly!

In fact, the knight was in a secure position, thanks to a secret tactical resource. Therefore, Carlsen confidently grabs White's important central pawn.

16...♖xe4! 17 ♖e1? *(D)*

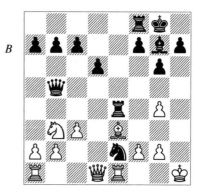

B

17...♕h5+! 0-1

Apparently, White had missed the simple checkmate 18 gxh5 ♖h4#. In retrospect, one can claim that White's idea of trapping the besieged knight could have been put into practice after 16 a4, as this forces the black queen off the 5th rank: after 16...♕a6 17 ♗e3 ♖xe4 18 ♖e1 ♖xe3!? 19 fxe3 ♘xc3!? 20 bxc3 ♗xc3 the position is quite unclear. Alas...

The Rook's Breathtaking Performance

Game 47
Erdogdu – Shanava
Istanbul 2004
Nimzowitsch Defence

1 e4 ♘c6

The *Nimzowitsch Defence*. With this offbeat (yet modern) system, Black allows his opponent to build a broad centre with 2 d4 if he wishes. Still, careless play from White might suddenly leave him with major problems, and White more often adopts the more modest reply seen in this game.

2 ♘f3 d6

With this move, the Georgian master steers the game towards Pirc waters. Instead, 2...d5 3 exd5 ♕xd5 4 ♘c3 gives the game a more

concrete character: 4...♕h5 5 ♘b5! (targeting the vulnerable c7-pawn) or 4...♕a5 5 ♗b5! (to prevent Black's light-squared bishop from taking an active role on g4).

3 d4 ♘f6 4 ♘c3 ♗g4 5 ♗b5

Curiously enough, White skips normal development with ♗e2. More ambitiously, he aims to neutralize his opponent's pressure on d4 by pinning the c6-knight.

5...a6 6 ♗xc6+ bxc6 7 h3 ♗h5 8 ♕e2 *(D)*

A silent declaration: while giving priority to other goals, Black has ignored his dark-squared

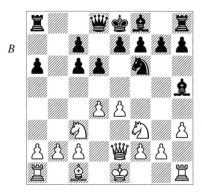

bishop's development. Therefore for the moment, his king is stuck in the centre. With his queen's 'little move', Erdogdu prepares to castle queenside. The text-move might also help White achieve the e5 advance in some variations. Of course, there are also some risks. The half-open b-file, and especially the b2-square, might turn into a target for Black's pieces. However, Black is not at present in a position to launch an attack.

8...e6 9 g4!

White's decision to castle queenside makes this advance a part of an effective plan, rather than an unfounded attack. This way, White has gained some space on the kingside and also stranded Black's light-squared bishop out of play for some time at least.

9...&g6 10 &g5 &b8!? (D)

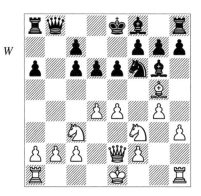

À la Kožul! Lately, Croatian grandmaster Zdenko Kožul's Variation (1 e4 c5 2 ♘f3 ♘c6 3 d4 cxd4 4 ♘xd4 ♘f6 5 ♘c3 d6 6 &g5 e6 7 ♕d2 a6 8 0-0-0 &d7) against the Richter-Rauzer has been a topical way for Black to handle the Open Sicilian. Here, similarly enough, Black allows

his opponent to capture on f6. In return for his shattered pawn-structure, he aims to generate direct pressure via the half-open b-file. Black would acquire a great many pawns in the centre after 11 &xf6 gxf6 and this makes Shanava's approach similar to Kožul's idea.

11 0-0-0 ♕b6 12 ♘d2! (D)

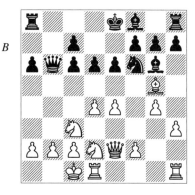

It seems odd to retreat during the height of the battle, but the knight aims to land powerfully on the c4-square, where it neutralizes the black queen's pressure on b2. Also, trapping the bishop with the upcoming march of the f-pawn has now become a concrete threat. In his turn, Black has to find an answer to this critical question: is it possible to capture the loose pawn, or is d4 poisoned?

12...♕xd4

Raising the stakes. In fact, Black had few viable options, since a routine continuation like 12...&e7 13 f4 ♖b8 14 ♘b3 would leave him in a precarious situation.

13 ♘c4?!

Wasn't it possible to lock up the bishop directly with 13 f4! instead? Indeed it was, but putting the knight on a very effective square with tempo also looks attractive.

13...♕c5

Attacking the bishop.

14 f4

At first glance, it might appear that Black is under severe pressure. The continual threats have prevented Shanava from completing his development, especially on the kingside. But Black finds a tactical solution to the problem of his light-squared bishop.

14...♘xe4!? 15 ♘xe4 &xe4 16 ♕xe4 d5 (D)

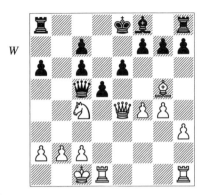

This idea has its logic. Now White has to give back his extra material, but some calculation is in order here to find the best way forward.

17 ♕e5!

Centralization is very effective, as usual. It was not possible to hold on to the extra material, but at least Erdogdu wants to grab the loose c7-pawn in return.

17...♕xc4 18 ♕xc7 *(D)*

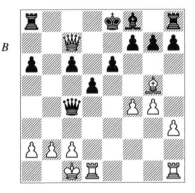

So, White's army is getting closer to Black's king. At the same time, White now has total control over d8, and his pressure against the c6-pawn has more or less immobilized Black's queen. All these considerations make the position very difficult for Black. But Shanava now finds a very interesting idea.

18...♗a3?

A spectacular move. Black assesses that the core problem is his king's position, so he wants to clear its path to castling in the quickest way possible. At the same time, he creates some discomfort for White's own king.

However, it turns out that White has a strong answer, and that Black's best chance lay in

18...a5!, the key idea being that ...♕a6 is then available as a vital defensive resource (e.g. 19 ♖d4 ♕a6 or 19 ♕b7 ♕a6). After 19 ♖he1 ♗b4 20 a3 0-0 21 axb4 axb4, the game is unclear, as Black has evacuated his king and possesses two pawns and counterplay for the piece. 19 a3 ♕a6 20 ♕e5 c5 21 ♖he1 (21 ♖xd5 f6) 21...♕d6 also sees Black holding his game together.

19 ♖d4!! *(D)*

19 bxa3 0-0 is less clear, as White's king would be vulnerable to various attacks from Black's forces.

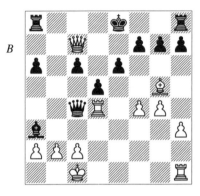

Actually, this inspiring rook-lift promotes White's attack in a different manner (deflection!) from what we're accustomed to witnessing. Of course, the rook is taboo: it's checkmate after 19...♕xd4? 20 ♕xc6+ ♔f8 21 ♕xa8#. Still, Black can fight on.

19...♗xb2+?

Just at the most exciting moment, Black collapses. We shall return to the game shortly afterwards, but first answer this question: what would White play after the dangerous-looking 19...♕c3? Believe it or not, 20 ♖b4!! *(D)*.

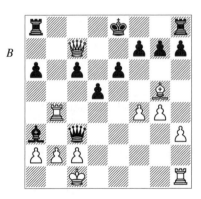

This move with an interference theme threatens mate in one: 21 ♕e7#!

Once again, 20...♕xb4? loses to 21 ♕xc6+, and after the continuation 20...♗xb4? 21 bxc3 Black is material down. So, it's obvious that Black's only chance is to secure his king by castling (finally!): 20...0-0. But now the cold-blooded 21 ♖b3! gives White a substantial advantage: 21...♗xb2+ 22 ♔b1! (much better than 22 ♖xb2 ♕f3, which would leave White's rooks uncoordinated).

So what can we suggest for Black? Probably the best practical try is 19...♕c5. Still, I believe that after 20 bxa3 (this capture is forced) 20...♕xa3+ 21 ♔b1 0-0 22 ♖d3!, the rook will handle the security issues once it finds time to land on b3.

20 ♔b1 ♕c5 *(D)*

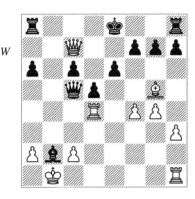

W

Now the decisive strike justifiably belongs to the star of the battle.

21 ♖xd5! 1-0

Black resigned as the other rook will decisively join the assault after 21...exd5 22 ♖e1+. What a breathtaking performance!

Piece-Play on the Kingside

Game 48

D. Howell – Ashton

British Rapidplay Ch, Halifax 2008

Two Knights Defence

1 e4 e5 2 ♘f3 ♘c6 3 ♗c4 ♘f6

This is the *Two Knights Defence*. In this opening, Black allows his opponent to target f7 directly with 4 ♘g5. But in compensation, he prevents White's plan of c3 and d4 by attacking e4 for the moment. Pros and cons...

4 d3

Historically speaking, 4 ♘g5 d5 (4...♗c5 is the *Traxler Counter-Gambit*) 5 exd5 ♘a5 (even 5...b5 is possible) 6 ♗b5+ c6 7 dxc6 bxc6 8 ♗e2 is an ever-lasting theoretical discussion between two opposing opinions: White's extra pawn vs Black's lead in development.

However, nowadays many chess-players prefer to avoid highly theoretical battles, and opt for unforced manoeuvring play instead. The reason for this approach is that it is very difficult to get a significant edge in a forcing line against a well-prepared opponent. That's exactly why the Closed System with 4 d3 is becoming more and more popular.

4...♗c5 *(D)*

Black locates his bishop actively on the a7-g1 diagonal, and that's very natural. Still, alternatives such as 4...♗e7 and even 4...h6!? are possible.

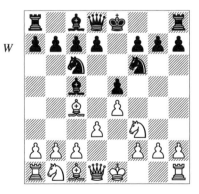

W

5 c3 a6

Seemingly rather odd, this advance is quite popular. White's plan of c3, followed by the d4 advance at a suitable moment, will force the bishop to find another square. Therefore, Black prepares to tuck his bishop into a7.

6 ♗b3

A second move from an already-developed bishop also strikes one as curious. The retreat is based on concrete grounds: with the bishop on c4, Black's ...d5 advance will have to be answered with exd5. With the bishop at a safe distance on b3, White will be able to maintain his pawn on e4. White will also be able to preserve his bishop from exchange in the event of a later ...♘a5.

6...♗a7 7 h3!?

Usually, it is difficult to claim any real edge after making so many preparatory moves. But White has a clear idea in mind, and therefore prevents moves such as ...♘g4, which would disrupt White's planned manoeuvres.

7...d6 8 ♘bd2 0-0 *(D)*

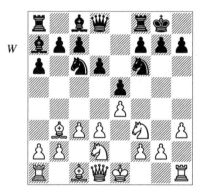

9 ♘f1!

This is the reason why White has delayed castling for so many moves: if he had previously castled, then his desired manoeuvre ♘bd2-f1-g3/e3 could only be employed after ♖e1 (which not only costs a move, but may not be the best square for the rook). But Howell delays castling for a few moves, and thereby saves time.

9...d5

Of course, ♘f1 was also a retreating move, which encourages Black to land a central counterblow at this precise moment. Now Black has a positional threat: once again, ...dxe4 followed by ...♕xd1+ would create an equal, dull position. Thus White has to neutralize this plan.

10 ♕e2!

It wasn't possible to stop the opening of the d-file any more, but at least White can avoid the exchange of queens. White's chances of claiming an edge are tied up with his kingside attack. Without queens on the board, White's attacking possibilities would be severely limited.

10...dxe4 11 dxe4 ♕e7 12 ♘g3

The manoeuvre is completed at last. White is now ready to castle and initiate his kingside play.

12...h6?! *(D)*

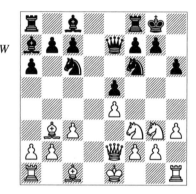

Unforced, aimless pawn moves in front of a king weaken the control over some squares, and turn the pawn into a target for the enemy pieces. Apparently, Black doesn't want his opponent to create a discomforting pin on f6 with ♗g5 followed by ♘h5. But because of this superficial thought, suddenly bigger problems arise.

13 ♘h4!

Why is White once again abandoning the plan of castling? Changing circumstances might give us more promising opportunities, so it's best to be flexible. With this thematic manoeuvre, White aims to place a knight on f5 and also threatens a knight fork on g6.

13...♔h7 14 ♘hf5

We shall very soon see that the white knight on f5 has a very critical role in the kingside attack.

14...♕e8 15 ♕f3!

Since 12...h6?!, the course of the battle has been like this: threat – defence – another threat. It is obvious that Black will not manage to survive by continuing this routine. With his last move, White is threatening to win a pawn with ♘xh6 followed by ♕xf6.

15...♘g8 *(D)*

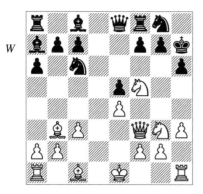

White's kingside activity has become extreme. He should now be looking for a concrete tactical blow to exploit his large local superiority of force.

16 ♘xg7!

Young grandmaster Howell initiates the decisive sequence. Black's pawn-structure is torn apart with this knight sacrifice.

16...♔xg7 17 ♘h5+ 1-0

Checkmate is inevitable after 17...♔h7 (or 17...♔h8) 18 ♕g3, while 17...♔g6 18 ♕g3+! ♔xh5 19 ♗d1+ (don't forget the light-squared bishop!) 19...♗g4 20 ♕xg4# is a different form of checkmate.

The Power of the Zwischenzug

Game 49

J. Friedel – De Jong

Hoogeveen 2009

Sicilian Defence

1 e4 c5 2 ♘f3 e6 3 d4 cxd4 4 ♘xd4 a6 *(D)*

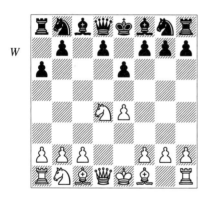

This is the *Kan Variation*. With this flexible system against the Open Sicilian, Black aims to restrain White's knights, and prepares a timely ...b5-b4 combined with pressure against White's central structure.

5 ♘c3 b5

Showing his hand: Black gives priority to developing his queenside pieces. While it directly targets the centre, this approach entails some risk as Black is a long way from castling, and so far has no pieces developed.

6 ♗d3 ♗b7 7 0-0

On the other hand, White has developed his kingside forces first and promptly castled.

7...♘c6 8 ♘xc6

Of course, it was completely OK to support the knight with 8 ♗e3, but apparently Friedel prefers to develop more freely.

8...♗xc6 9 ♕e2 *(D)*

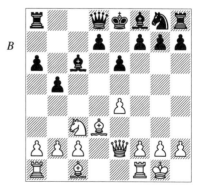

A step towards connecting the rooks, this move also toys with the thematic ♘d5 idea, which can be useful in some variations.

9...♗c5 10 ♗e3 d6

Capturing with 10...♗xe3 is also possible, but exchanging dark-squared bishops would cause some problems on the dark squares for Black, since he has already placed nearly all his pawns on light squares.

11 a4

Increasing the tension: in addition to the opposing bishops, now there is a direct contact between the a- and b-pawns.

11...♗xe3? *(D)*

The fundamental idea behind ♕e2 would be seen clearly after 11...b4 12 ♘d5!. In that case, the pressure on a6 does not allow the natural 12...♘e7 since White replies 13 ♘xe7 ♔xe7 (13...♕xe7 14 ♗xc5 dxc5 15 ♗xa6) 14 ♗xc5 dxc5 15 ♕h5! (15 ♗xa6 ♕d4 would give an unclear position) 15...♕b6 16 a5!. After 12...♗b7, White's knight would find a good square: 13 ♗xc5 dxc5 14 ♘e3 followed by ♘c4.

Considering these dangerous lines, Black decided the text-move would be safest. But a surprise awaits him.

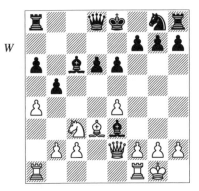

12 axb5!

This unexpected *zwischenzug* (in-between move) leaves two black pieces under attack, and suddenly sharpens the game.

12...axb5 13 ♗xb5

As the bishop on c6 is hanging once again, White can still delay the recapture on e3.

13...♗xb5

Apparently, De Jong understands that he has lost a pawn thanks to the zwischenzug, and he seeks at least to damage White's pawn-structure. That's why he preferred the text-move over 13...♖c8 or 13...♘e7.

14 ♕xb5+ ♔f8 15 fxe3 *(D)*

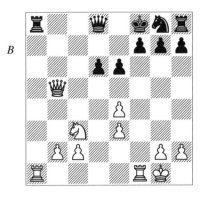

After so many exchanges, the position has simplified somewhat. In the process, White has won a pawn and deprived Black of his castling rights. On the other hand, his pawn-structure has been damaged after fxe3. Quite interestingly, White's claim of an advantage in this position is not based on material factors. His temporary (but significant) trumps in terms of his opponent's weak king and play on the f-file are more important. On the other hand, Black's hopes are grounded on White's structural defects. A splendid clash of *static* and *dynamic* elements, isn't it?

15...♖b8

Understandably, being a pawn down, De Jong avoids further exchanges and puts his rook on the b-file with tempo.

16 ♖a7!

Zwischenzug number 2! There is a guiding element in this position: doubled pawns give their possessor opportunities on the half-open file. With the aid of the zwischenzug, Friedel connects his play on the seventh rank and the f-file. Just to make sure, let's analyse the consequences of accepting the 'gift': 16...♖xb5?! 17 ♖axf7+ ♔e8 18 ♖f8+ ♔d7 (18...♔e7 19 ♖1f7#) 19 ♖xd8+ ♔xd8 20 ♘xb5 and White heads to the endgame two pawns up.

Therefore, Black decides to meet the pressure on the f-file by (finally!) developing his knight.

16...♘f6 17 ♖xf6! *(D)*

White can again leave his queen *en prise* thanks to the attack upon f7: after 17...♖xb5 18 ♖fxf7+ (this time capturing with the other rook) followed by 19 ♘xb5 it is difficult to propose even a single constructive move for Black.

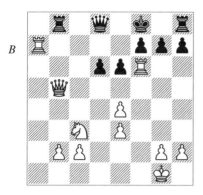

17...gxf6

There is no choice, since recapturing with the queen would leave the rook hanging.

18 ♕h5

White consistently pursues his pressure on the f7-square. Tactics have been White's real helpers throughout the game, but ever since 11 a4, his principal strategy has been 'play on the open files'.

18...♕e8 *(D)*

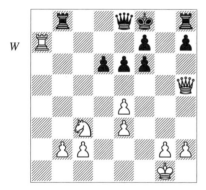

Here we come to the *critical moment*! In a chess battle, sometimes there occurs a climax of the fight. At this moment, it's crucial to make the right decision, since anything less than the very best move might undo all the previous good work. So far, White has used almost all his forces to press against his opponent's Achilles' Heel, f7. Now, in order to increase the pressure, Friedel needs to bring up the reserves. The queen and rook are ideally located, but the knight has been just a spectator. Sometimes, improving the position of such a piece has decisive consequences.

19 e5!

A great *square-clearance* sacrifice! The knight will be transferred to e4, and afterwards the simple ♘f6(+) idea will leave Black helpless. Black has a variety of options, none of which bring relief: 19...dxe5 (or 19...fxe5) 20 ♕h6+ ♚g8 21 ♘e4, 19...f5 20 exd6, followed by 21 ♖e7, and 19...d5 20 ♕h6+ ♚g8 21 exf6 are winning for White. In these variations, the major cause of Black's problems is the white queen's penetration via h6, so De Jong decides to prevent this idea.

19...h6 *(D)*

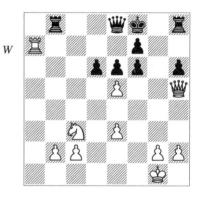

20 exf6?!

The new threat is 21 ♖e7. That said, the planned 20 ♘e4! is a neater way to win.

20...♖h7 21 ♘e4 *(D)*

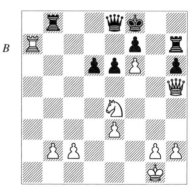

White aims to increase the pressure on f7 by ♘xd6. Since 19 e5!, the course of the game has been another example of the 'threat – defence – another threat' cycle. At some point, one side will exhaust his resources: either the initiative burns itself out, or the defence collapses. Black's scattered pieces against White's harmonious forces are the main reason why the latter outcome applies here.

21...♛d8?

21...♛c6 is much more resilient.

22 ♘g5!

A great strike, benefiting from the loose rook.

22...hxg5 23 ♖xf7+! 1-0

A fitting end for this outstanding battle: 23...♖xf7 24 ♛h8#!

A Terrifying (K)nightmare!

Game 50
Rublevsky – E. Zude
European Ch, Aix-les-Bains 2011
Sicilian Defence

1 e4 c5 2 ♘f3 d6 3 d4 cxd4 4 ♘xd4 ♘f6 5 ♘c3 a6 6 ♗c4 (D)

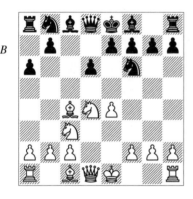

In the *Sozin Attack* against Black's Najdorf Sicilian, White aggressively deploys his bishop on the a2-g8 diagonal.

6...e6

With the white bishop on c4, it would be illogical for Black to make the ...e5 advance (which is quite standard in many Najdorf lines). Zude aims to limit the bishop.

7 ♗b3 b5 8 0-0 ♗e7

Wouldn't it be more natural to follow up with ...♗b7 after ...b5? It might be, but don't forget the risks of postponing the development of the kingside. In a probable variation, 8...♗b7 9 ♖e1 (with ♘d5 ideas) 9...♗e7? 10 ♗xe6! fxe6 11 ♘xe6 ♛d7 12 ♘xg7+ ♔f7 13 ♘f5, White has a dangerous attack. This typical Sicilian sacrifice once again shows the risks of delaying castling.

9 ♛f3 ♛b6

As previously mentioned, continuing development with ...♗b7 actually invites the sacrifice on e6. Therefore, Black's move-order looks very logical. Now 10 e5? cannot cause a serious headache, as Black has 10...♗b7 in reply.

10 ♗e3 ♛b7 11 ♛g3 0-0 (D)

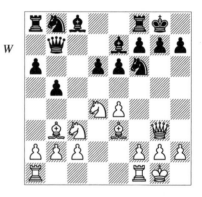

With careful play, Black has managed to complete his kingside development. Still, as White's pieces are more active, he thinks that he is already prepared for an attack on this side of the board. Rublevsky wants to see how Black will deploy his queenside pieces, and meanwhile brings his rooks to the central files before initiating any direct action.

12 ♗h6 ♘e8 13 ♖fe1 ♗d7

Nowadays, immediately releasing the pressure on g7 by 13...♔h8 is seen more often. Apparently, Zude thinks that he has sufficiently covered g7, and continues with his queenside plan. Unfortunately, this allows another enterprising idea from White.

14 ♖ad1 ♞c6 *(D)*

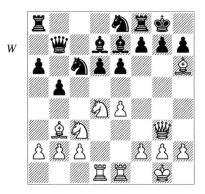

Finally, Black has completed his queenside development. But the looseness of the bishop on e7 allows White to fast-track his forces to the kingside by tactical means.

15 ♘d5!

Sacrifices with ♘d5 and ♘f5 are very typical in the Open Sicilian. Now, accepting the sacrifice is questionable: 15...exd5?! 16 ♘xc6! (it's important that this capture comes with a threat) 16...♗f6 (after 16...♘xc6 17 exd5 both bishops are under attack, while 16...♕xc6 17 exd5 leaves the e7-bishop hanging) 17 exd5. Note that it's not possible for Black to win a pawn on c6, since White wins material after 17...♗xc6 18 dxc6 ♕xc6 19 ♗d5.

Black, therefore, unwillingly seeks salvation by securing his bishop on a different square.

15...♗d8 16 ♘f5! *(D)*

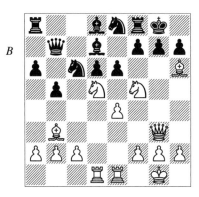

What a terrifying (k)nightmare! Although Black has removed his bishop from the e-file, he cannot avoid all dangers on this file. Thanks to a tactical resource (after accepting the sacrifice,

a dangerous idea – ♖xe8 followed by ♕xg7# – suddenly emerges) White can leave both his knights *en prise*.

16...exf5

In order to neutralize the pressure, it is obligatory to eliminate White's menacing knight on f5.

17 exf5 ♘e5 *(D)*

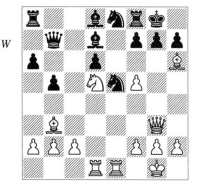

The knight aims to help in the defence by preventing the ♖xe8 and ♕xg7# idea. However, Rublevsky rises to the occasion.

18 ♖xe5!

Not allowing Black a single quiet moment! This exchange sacrifice pursues the initiative with the utmost vigour. Having sacrificed material, this is precisely the right type of approach.

18...dxe5 19 f6 g6 *(D)*

The unbearable pressure on g7 forces Black to make this advance. But to no avail...

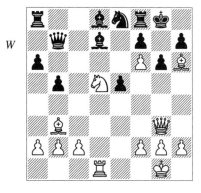

20 ♘e7+ 1-0

A wonderful example of how effective the thematic ♘d5 and ♘f5 sacrifices can be in the Open Sicilian.

A Petroff Classic

Game 51
Anand – Kasimdzhanov
Rapid match (3), Tashkent 2011
Petroff Defence

1 e4 e5 2 ♘f3 ♘f6 *(D)*

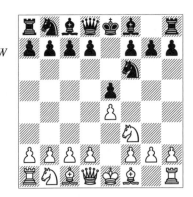

The *Petroff Defence*. This solid system gives Black fairly good chances of equalizing. Instead of defending his e-pawn, Black counter-attacks against White's own e-pawn. The elimination of these two pawns tends to limit the attacking opportunities for both sides, and an open e-file often proves an avenue for exchanges of the major pieces.

Of course, just like all other opening systems, it isn't possible to express all the details of this rich defence in a single paragraph. Anand opts for a line with opposite-side castling, as this might give him more chances for a successful attack.

3 ♘xe5 d6 4 ♘f3 ♘xe4 5 ♘c3

The main continuation here is 5 d4. However, with the text-move, White aims to break the symmetry, by somewhat altering the pawn-structure.

5...♘xc3 6 dxc3 ♗e7 7 ♗e3 ♘c6

Without wasting any time, both sides continue to develop their pieces. It seems like the queenside is the right place for White's king, since his doubled pawns make this side of the board more secure.

8 ♕d2 0-0

In the previous comment, we noted that the white king's likely position is more or less clear. But Black's decision regarding the position of his own king will greatly shape the further course of the game. What would you recommend? Adventurously castling kingside, or more solidly castling queenside? There isn't a right or wrong answer to this question; just like opening preferences, the decision will be based on one's own taste. After ...0-0-0, as both sides have placed their kings on the same side, attacking the king will not be the base element. Contrarily after ...0-0, a sharper struggle awaits both sides. As White's extra pawn in front of his king makes his position a little bit safer, it is possible to claim that White has a slight practical edge.

9 0-0-0 *(D)*

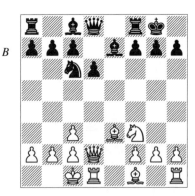

9...♘e5 10 ♔b1

Very often this is a useful little move. While sidestepping from the loose c1-h6 diagonal, the king is also taking care of a2. Anand wishes to see his opponent's set-up before deciding how to deploy his own forces, and therefore makes a useful semi-waiting move.

10...c6

Apparently, opening the g-file with 10...♘xf3 did not appeal to the Uzbek player.

11 ♗e2 *(D)*

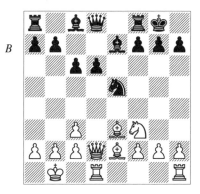

11...♘g4

Kasimdzhanov's plan was not to exchange knights; instead, he tries to acquire the bishop-pair.

12 ♗d3

White probably has little choice but to allow the exchange of the bishop. But the following line in which he seeks to extract a half-open h-file as the price for this seems like a reasonable choice: 12 ♗d4 c5 (otherwise the knight would have to retreat after White plays h3) 13 h3!? cxd4 14 hxg4 dxc3 15 ♕xc3 ♗xg4. Maybe Anand looked at this concrete variation, but was unimpressed by the compensation for the pawn.

12...d5?!

Of course, it is important to solve the problem of the vulnerable d-pawn, and to take action in the centre. But wouldn't it be more logical to continue with 'b', after saying 'a'? Black should have removed a possible attacking weapon and acquired the bishop-pair by 12...♘xe3.

13 ♗f4

Taking the opportunity to preserve the bishop.

13...♗d6 14 h3!

The game has had a calm start, but the tension is increasing step by step. After the capture on f4, won't a knight fork be possible on f2?

14...♗xf4

Of course not! Anand is well aware of the dangers awaiting his opponent on the h-file. He benefits from this element by rushing his pieces to the kingside.

15 ♗xh7+!! *(D)*

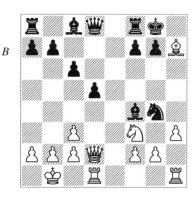

A long and forced sequence of moves begins.

15...♔h8

As White would have the upper hand after 15...♔xh7 16 hxg4+ ♗h6 17 g5, Black's reply is forced.

16 ♕xf4 ♘xf2 17 ♘g5! *(D)*

White thinks that he has enough firepower on the kingside, and therefore is not worried about losing an exchange. Black has to be very careful now, as White's ♕h4 idea is highly menacing.

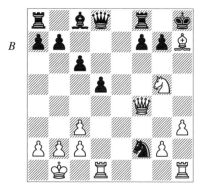

17...f6?!

A very natural response, but this defensive idea proves insufficient after White's marvellous reply. 17...♕f6 is more resilient. After 18 ♕h4 ♕h6 (meeting the queen's manoeuvre) 19 ♕xf2 ♗xg5 20 ♗d3 White still has the upper hand, with a more secure king and more active pieces, but the game is far from over.

Could Anand manage to prove the dubiousness of Black's last move? No question about that!

18 ♘f7+!

An effective way to prevent 18...fxg5. So as not to lose decisive material immediately, the knight has to be removed.

18...Ɍxf7 19 ♗g6 ♘xd1 *(D)*

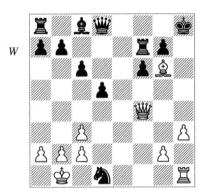

At the moment, Black has an extra rook and knight(!) after accepting all the gifts. But checkmate outweighs everything else.

20 ♕h4+ ♔g8 21 Ɍe1! *(D)*

Obviously, it was very important not to allow Black's king to run away. But here, the move-order has a crucial impact on the result of the battle. Although 21 ♕h7+?! ♔f8 22 Ɍe1 seems similar, it is insufficient for victory: 22...♘xc3+! 23 bxc3 (otherwise the knight would prepare his

king's escape by closing the file with ...♘e4) 23...♗e6! (Black blocks the e-file, and forces his opponent to weaken his first rank) 24 Ɍxe6 ♕b6+ 25 ♔c1 ♕g1+ and Black draws by perpetual check.

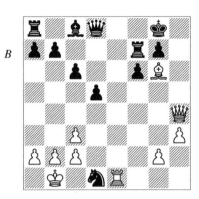

Anand's accurate play right to the end makes this miniature a real Petroff classic.

21...♘xc3+ 22 bxc3 ♗e6 23 Ɍxe6 ♕b6+ 24 ♔c1 1-0

The same ingredients, but here Black resigns. Why? Because White's queen controls e1 from the h4-square, and therefore does not allow his opponent to benefit from the weakness of his back rank: 24...♕g1+ 25 Ɍe1 and White wins.

The Duel of the Veterans

Game 52

Cebalo – Vasiukov

European Seniors Team Ch, Šibenik 2014

Dutch Defence

1 d4 f5 2 ♗g5!?

This odd-looking bishop move is a blood-thirsty reply to the *Dutch Defence* (1 d4 f5). In common with the Trompowsky Attack (1 d4 ♘f6 2 ♗g5), here White aims to spoil Black's pawn-structure: if Black continues simple king-side development with 2...♘f6, White can reply 3 ♗xf6. But what if Black delays his development, and disturbs the bishop with 2...h6 instead? Of course, it is not possible to trap and win the bishop so easily, since traces of the Fool's Mate theme emerge: 3 ♗h4 g5 4 e3 (the

aggressive 4 e4 is also perfectly playable, as is 4 ♗g3, since 4...f4? fails to 5 e3) 4...gxh4?? 5 ♕h5#. Certainly this is just an illustrative variation. Nevertheless, with his provocative treatment of the ever-dangerous Dutch Defence, White aims to carry the game into somewhat unorthodox waters.

2...g6

Not surprisingly, this is the main variation against White's 2 ♗g5. As his e-pawn is currently pinned, Black prepares to develop his dark-squared bishop on the long diagonal.

3 e3 ♘h6?!

But this knight manoeuvre may be a little too eccentric. Black should prefer faster development with 3...♗g7, in order to get his king into safety.

4 h4!? *(D)*

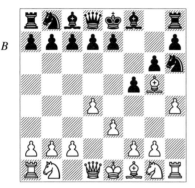

Pawn-chains are an important strategic aspect of chess, and have been a subject of debate among chess-players ever since Nimzowitsch discussed them systematically in his writings. Although they form a solid structure, the pawns' static positioning makes them vulnerable to attack from the enemy pawns (know as *pawn-levers*). In this case, the further advance to h5 is an important idea to which Black must be constantly alert.

4...♘f7

In response, Black completes his knight manoeuvre and for the moment prevents h5 by attacking the bishop.

5 ♗f4 d6 6 ♘f3 ♘d7?! *(D)*

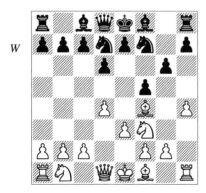

In his excellent instructive work *How to Beat Your Dad at Chess,* Murray Chandler devotes

considerable attention to bishop sacrifices on f7. He states: "The f7-square is Black's most vulnerable point prior to castling. However, Black's *lack* of development is not the primary cause of 'accidents' on this square. *Awkward* piece placement is the main reason." This point couldn't be explained better. Experienced grandmaster Vasiukov is of course very well aware of this. Nevertheless, he underestimates the dangers that will be caused by the bishop's deployment on c4. After 6...♘d7?!, Black's light-squared bishop's diagonal has been obstructed, and this severely weakens e6. White duly replies...

7 ♗c4! ♗g7?

No, this time it's *not* better late than never!

8 ♗xf7+!

With the intention of luring the king to the centre, and thereby exposing it to the attacks of White's various forces.

8...♔xf7 9 ♘g5+ ♔f6

A sad necessity. Other king moves fail as follows: after 9...♔e8 (or 9...♔f8), the queen is lost to 10 ♘e6 (using the weakened e6-square as an outpost), while against 9...♔g8, White wins at least an exchange by 10 ♘e6 ♕e8 11 ♘xc7 ♕d8 12 ♘xa8.

10 ♘c3

Threatening mate in one (11 ♘d5#). That's quite brutal, but what can you expect with such an exposed king?

10...c6 *(D)*

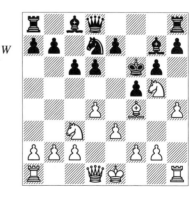

11 ♕f3!

After the first mating threat has been fended off, Cebalo introduces another deadly threat with this extraordinary queen move. The idea is

12 ♘ce4+! (in order to open the f-file) 12...fxe4 13 ♗e5# – a neat example of double check.

How should Black deal with this dangerous idea? Pinning the knight with 11...♕a5 may be the best try, but after 12 e4 (here the idea is 13 e5+! dxe5 14 ♗d2, unpinning the knight and threatening ♘ce4#), White has an undisputed pull. Instead, Vasiukov decides to clear e7 as a flight-square.

11...e5 12 ♕d5!! *(D)*

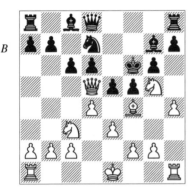

Let me make an ambitious bet: the central square d5 has never been used as effectively as it is here! Her majesty is untouchable due to the checkmate (12...cxd5 13 ♘xd5#), and now the threats on e6 and f7 are simply unbearable.

12...♕e7 *(D)*

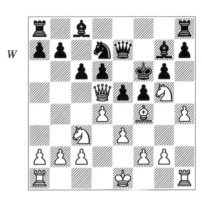

Preventing both threats simultaneously, but now e7 is blocked, and Cebalo decides matters from another point.

13 ♘xh7+! 1-0

A fitting beautiful finale (13...♖xh7 is met by 14 ♗g5#) to this short but exciting duel between two strong veteran players. Black handled the opening phase in an unusual manner, but unfortunately he was punished for his *awkward piece placement*.

Opera in St. Louis

Game 53

So – Kasparov

St. Louis blitz 2016

Modern Defence

Following his retirement from professional chess in 2005, Kasparov has not participated in regular tournament play. But when he has occasionally played exhibition games, he has shown some of his old magic, beating former world championship rivals Karpov (in 2009) and Short (in 2015). However, the 'Ultimate Blitz Challenge' in 2016 was a different level of contest: he faced the top three finishers in the US Championship, all of them in their twenties and current world top-ten players: World no. 2 Caruana, blitz demon Nakamura, and 22-year-old Wesley So.

The game presented here was the tournament's most memorable battle, and immediately hailed as a masterpiece by the on-site commentators: "Wesley's game against Kasparov will go down in history as one of the greatest blitz games ever played. I will remember that game for the rest of my life." (GM Yasser Seirawan). After his defeat, Kasparov ruefully stated: "It reminded me of the games Morphy played with amateurs ... I was an amateur in this game!"

1 ♘f3 g6 2 e4 ♗g7 3 d4 d6 4 c4

By a slightly unusual move-order, White invites his opponent to enter the waters of the

King's Indian (to which 4...♘f6 5 ♘c3 would now transpose). But Kasparov chooses a different path:

4...♗g4

The bishop's sortie puts pressure on the d4-pawn, making use of the knight's absence from f6.

5 ♗e2 ♘c6 6 ♘bd2!? *(D)*

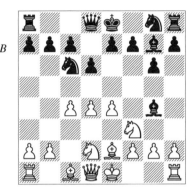

This indirect defence of the pawn is based on an 'elastic band' tactic: for the moment, it's not possible to grab the pawn, since 6...♘xd4?? costs Black a piece after 7 ♘xd4 ♗xe2 8 ♘xe2.

6...e5 7 d5 ♘ce7

The seemingly more active 7...♘d4?? similarly loses a piece to 8 ♘xd4. That's why the knight retreats.

8 h3 ♗d7

The light-squared bishop is an important piece in this type of structure. Not only is it Black's 'good' bishop, but in lines where Black launches a kingside pawn-storm, it plays a vital role in Black's attacking plans. Therefore he preserves this piece, rather than exchange it on f3.

After the text-move, the position looks like a King's Indian where White's knight is unusually placed on d2 rather than c3. If White now develops in standard fashion, this difference could work in Black's favour. But Wesley So finds a convincing way to put this knight to use right away:

9 c5!

Exerting pressure on d6 as well as clearing c4 for the knight. Since the knight is heading to c4 in any case, Kasparov decides to accept the pawn.

9...dxc5 10 ♘c4 f6 11 d6?! *(D)*

White pursues the initiative without pausing for breath. This is the right approach in principle, but 11 ♗e3! is more accurate, in order to force 11...b6. Then White can transpose to the game continuation with 12 d6 ♘c8, but an even better option is 12 b4!, when both 12...b5 13 ♘a5 and 12...cxb4 13 d6 ♘c8 14 dxc7 ♕xc7 15 ♖c1 are rather difficult for Black. Of course, to see all this in a blitz game is unrealistic, but it does show that White's decision on move 9 was fully correct.

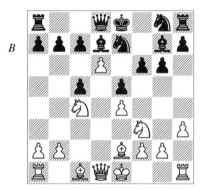

11...♘c8 12 ♗e3 b6?!

Black chooses the 'safe' option, which is a natural reflex when under attack and short of time. But the more assertive 12...b5! puts the onus on White to show he has enough compensation. After 13 dxc7 ♕xc7 14 ♘a3, he can create enough queenside play to stop Black simply consolidating.

13 0-0 ♗c6?!

13...♘h6? fails to 14 ♘cxe5! fxe5? 15 ♗g5. However, exchanging some pieces to neutralize White's pressure keeps Black very much in the game: 13...♘xd6 14 ♘xd6+ cxd6 15 ♕xd6 ♕e7 and after 16 ♕d2! (covering h6) 16...♖d8 17 ♕c1, Black's problems developing his kingside mean that White has good compensation.

After Black's actual choice, White whips up a devastating initiative with power play.

14 dxc7 ♕xc7 15 b4!

White sacrifices a pawn to open lines against the uncastled black king. From Kasparov's body language, it was clear that he understood that he was in deep trouble – after all, he was on the other side of such attacks many times in his career. But here, knowing what is about to hit you doesn't make it any easier to avoid it.

15...cxb4?

15...b5 was the last chance to make a fight of it, but White has a pleasant choice between 16 ♘a5 c4 17 a4 a6 18 ♕c2, with pressure, and the more dramatic 16 ♘cxe5 fxe5 17 ♗xc5, with excellent play for the piece.

16 ♖c1

Improving the rook's position, as well as creating some pinning threats.

16...♘ge7 17 ♕b3 *(D)*

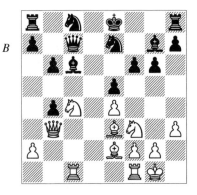

The discovered check ideas prevent Black from castling, and he is running very short of useful moves.

17...h6

Kasparov had seen that White was threatening 18 ♘cxe5! fxe5 19 ♘g5!, a deadly knight sortie. Even in a bad position, you can increase the chances of a miracle save by at least parrying the opponent's most direct threats.

18 ♖fd1

White simply improves his pieces, while Black cannot do likewise.

18...b5

This is not a case of 'better late than never', though Black had no answer to White's many threats, which included ♘h4 and ♘cxe5.

19 ♘cxe5!

While Black's uncoordinated pieces are scattered all over the board, White's forces act harmoniously together, and this makes the sacrifice easy to play. The first idea is to crank up the pressure on the pinned bishop on c6.

19...fxe5 20 ♗xb5 ♖b8 21 ♗a4! *(D)*

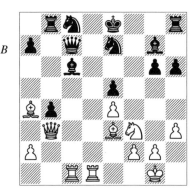

Calmly preserving the pin. Just like the position after White's 18th move, once again it is not possible to suggest a decent move for Black.

21...♕b7 22 ♖xc6!

À la Morphy! Remember his 13 ♖xd7! against the Duke and the Count in Game 3?

22...♘xc6 23 ♕e6+ ♘e7 24 ♗c5 *(D)*

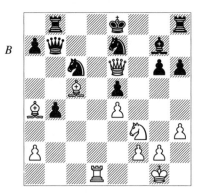

Total domination!

24...♖c8 25 ♗xe7 1-0

This is a fitting way to end our selection of miniatures. This game features the kind of dynamic play that we have seen many times throughout this book, together with the use of the initiative to punish slow development. These powerful methods can be used to defeat even the all-time greats of the game, and they are part of the essential toolkit of today's top players – Wesley So used little more than *two minutes* on this entire brilliant game!

Supplementary Games

Supplementary Game 1

Em. Lasker – J. Bauer

Amsterdam 1889
Bird's Opening

1 f4 d5 2 e3 ♘f6 3 b3 e6 4 ♗b2 ♗e7 5 ♗d3
b6 6 ♘f3 ♗b7 7 ♘c3 ♘bd7 8 0-0 0-0 9 ♘e2 c5
10 ♘g3 ♕c7 11 ♘e5 ♘xe5 12 ♗xe5 ♕c6 13
♕e2 a6 14 ♘h5 ♘xh5 *(D)*

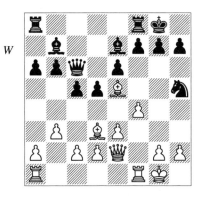

15 ♗xh7+ ♔xh7 16 ♕xh5+ ♔g8 17 ♗xg7
♔xg7 18 ♕g4+ ♔h7 19 ♖f3 e5 20 ♖h3+ ♕h6
21 ♖xh6+ ♔xh6 22 ♕d7 ♗f6 23 ♕xb7 ♔g7 24
♖f1 ♖ab8 25 ♕d7 ♖fd8 26 ♕g4+ ♔f8 27 fxe5
♗g7 28 e6 ♖b7 29 ♕g6 f6 30 ♖xf6+ ♗xf6 31
♕xf6+ ♔e8 32 ♕h8+ ♔e7 33 ♕g7+ ♔xe6 34
♕xb7 ♖d6 35 ♕xa6 d4 36 exd4 cxd4 37 h4 d3
38 ♕xd3 1-0

Supplementary Game 2

Nezhmetdinov – Chernikov

Rostov-on-Don 1962
Sicilian Defence

1 e4 c5 2 ♘f3 ♘c6 3 d4 cxd4 4 ♘xd4 g6 5
♘c3 ♗g7 6 ♗e3 ♘f6 7 ♗c4 0-0 8 ♗b3 ♘g4 9
♕xg4 ♘xd4 10 ♕h4 ♕a5 11 0-0 ♗f6 *(D)*

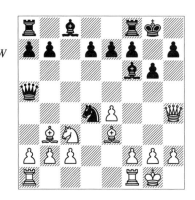

12 ♕xf6 ♘e2+ 13 ♘xe2 exf6 14 ♘c3 ♖e8
15 ♘d5 ♖e6 16 ♗d4 ♔g7 17 ♖ad1 d6 18 ♖d3
♗d7 19 ♖f3 ♗b5 20 ♗c3 ♕d8 21 ♘xf6 ♗e2
22 ♘xh7+ ♔g8 23 ♖h3 ♖e5 24 f4 ♗xf1 25
♔xf1 ♖c8 26 ♗d4 b5 27 ♘g5 ♖c7 28 ♗xf7+
♖xf7 29 ♖h8+ ♔xh8 30 ♘xf7+ ♔h7 31 ♘xd8
♖xe4 32 ♘c6 ♖xf4+ 33 ♔e2 1-0

Supplementary Game 3

Polugaevsky – Korchnoi

Candidates match (12), Buenos Aires 1980
Queen's Indian Defence

1 ♘f3 ♘f6 2 c4 b6 3 g3 e6 4 ♗g2 ♗b7 5 0-0
♗e7 6 d4 0-0 7 d5 exd5 8 ♘h4 c6 9 cxd5 ♘xd5
10 ♘f5 ♗c5 11 e4 ♘e7 12 ♘xg7 *(D)*

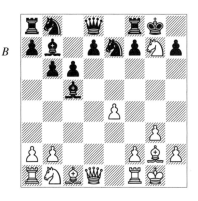

12...♔xg7 13 b4 ♗xb4 14 ♕d4+ f6 15 ♕xb4 c5 16 ♕d2 ♘bc6 17 ♗b2 ♗a6 18 ♖d1 ♘e5 19 ♘a3 ♘7c6 20 ♕e3 ♕e7 21 f4 ♘c4 22 ♘xc4 ♗xc4 23 e5 fxe5 24 ♗xc6 dxc6 25 ♖d7 ♕xd7 26 ♕xe5+ ♔f7 27 ♕f6+ ♔g8 28 ♕g5+ ♔f7 29 ♖e1 ♕e6 30 ♕g7+ ♔e8 31 ♖xe6+ ♗xe6 32 ♗f6 ♗f7 33 ♗g5 ♔d7 34 ♗h6 c4 35 ♕xh7 c5 (D)

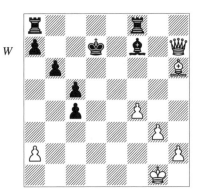

36 ♗xf8 ♖xf8 37 ♕g7 ♔e7 38 ♕e5+ ♔d7 39 g4 ♖e8 40 ♕f6 ♗d5 41 g5 ♖e2 42 h4 b5 43 ♕f5+ ♔d6 44 ♕f8+ ♔c6 45 ♕c8+ ♔d6 46 ♕d8+ ♔c6 47 ♕a8+ ♔d6 48 ♕f8+ ♔c6 49 a3 ♖e3 50 h5 c3 51 ♕f6+ ♗e6 52 ♔f2 c2 53 ♕b2 ♖h3 54 ♔g2 ♗f5 55 ♕f6+ ♔c7 56 ♕xf5 c1♕ 57 ♕e5+ ♔b6 58 ♔xh3 b4 59 axb4 cxb4 60 h6 ♕h1+ 61 ♔g4 ♕d1+ 62 ♔f5 ♕c2+ 63 ♔f6 b3 64 h7 ♕xh7 65 ♕e3+ ♔c6 66 ♕xb3 ♕h8+ 67 ♔e7 ♕h4 68 ♕c4+ ♔b6 69 ♕b4+ ♔c6 70 ♕e4+ ♔b5 71 ♔f7 a5 72 g6 ♕g4 73 ♕e5+ 1-0

Supplementary Game 4

Carlsen – Anand

World Ch match (2),
Sochi 2014
Ruy Lopez

1 e4 e5 2 ♘f3 ♘c6 3 ♗b5 ♘f6 4 d3 ♗c5 5 0-0 d6 6 ♖e1 0-0 7 ♗xc6 bxc6 8 h3 ♖e8 9 ♘bd2 ♘d7 10 ♘c4 ♗b6 11 a4 a5 12 ♘xb6 cxb6 13 d4 ♕c7 14 ♖a3 (D)

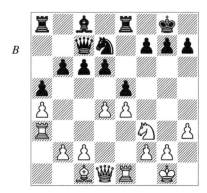

14...♘f8 15 dxe5 dxe5 16 ♘h4 ♖d8 17 ♕h5 f6 18 ♘f5 ♗e6 19 ♖g3 ♘g6 20 h4 ♗xf5 21 exf5 ♘f4 22 ♗xf4 exf4 23 ♖c3 c5 24 ♖e6 ♖ab8 25 ♖c4 ♕d7 26 ♔h2 ♖f8 27 ♖ce4 ♖b7 28 ♕e2 b5 29 b3 bxa4 30 bxa4 ♖b4 31 ♖e7 ♕d6 32 ♕f3 ♖xe4 33 ♕xe4 f3+ 34 g3 h5 35 ♕b7 1-0

Index of Players

Numbers refer to pages. A **bold** number means that the player had White.

Index of Openings

Numbers refer to pages.

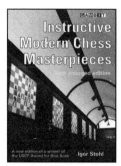

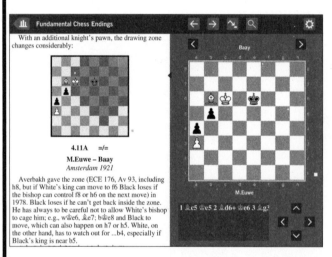